Do You Know Who I Am?!

Cartoons from *Mail & Guardian*, *Sunday Times* and *The Times*

Acknowledgements: *Thanks to my editors at the* Mail & Guardian *(Nic Dawes), at the* Sunday Times *(Ray Hartley, Mondli Makhanya) and at* The Times *(Phylicia Oppelt, Ray Hartley) and the production staff at all the newspapers; my website, ePublications and rights manager Richard Hainebach; my assistants Eleanora Bresler and Alecia Hartmann; Bridget Impey, Russell Martin and all at Jacana; Claudine Willatt-Bate; Nomalizo Ndlazi; and my family: Tevya, Nina and my wife Karina.*

10 Orange Street
Sunnyside
Auckland Park 2092
South Africa
(+27 11) 628-3200
www.jacana.co.za

in association with

2010 Jonathan Shapiro

All rights reserved

ISBN 978-1-77009-879-4

Cover design by Jonathan Shapiro

Page layout by Claudine Willatt-Bate
Printed by Creda Communications
Job No. 001349

See a complete list of Jacana titles at www.jacana.co.za

For fellow messengers

Other ZAPIRO books

The Madiba Years (1996)
The Hole Truth (1997)
End of Part One (1998)
Call Mr Delivery (1999)
The Devil Made Me Do It! (2000)
The ANC Went in 4x4 (2001)
Bushwhacked (2002)
Dr Do-Little and the African Potato (2003)
Long Walk to Free Time (2004)
Is There a Spin Doctor In the House? (2005)
Da Zuma Code (2006)
Take Two Veg and Call Me In the Morning (2007)
Pirates of Polokwane (2008)
Don't Mess With the President's Head (2009)

15 October 2009   Bafana Bafana's Brazilian coach, Joel Santana. Interpret this: eight losses in nine games.

Santana to be assessed by SA Football Association's new executive, headed by Kirsten Nematandani

18 October 2009

SAFA appoints three local coaches as advisors, fires Santana and calls for 'a Messiah'. Bafana's former (and even pricier) Brazilian coach drops a hint.

22 October 2009

Minister of Police and bodyguards run up a five-star hotel bill of nearly R600 000 – in his home town of Durban

At his inauguration as Free State University's first black vice-chancellor, Prof Jonathan Jansen drops charges against the four white students behind the infamous video showing black workers tricked into eating food the students had urinated on

22 October 2009

A well-meant gesture but with no apology demanded from the students or proper consultation of the victims

27 October 2009

In his first major speech as Finance Minister, Pravin Gordhan makes few concessions to an increasingly restless Left

29 October 2009

The ANC has lost its moral compass, says ANC veteran Kader Asmal, slamming the use of intemperate language to lobby for candidates (Julius Malema's 'kill for Zuma') or to deal with alleged criminals (Fikile Mbalula's 'shoot the bastards')

29 October 2009

MK military veterans tell Kader Asmal to go to the nearest cemetery and die. Prof Jonathan Jansen should be shot and killed for racism, says the ANC Youth League (they later 'clarify' that racism should be shot and killed).

After months of denials to his wife and the public, former Springbok star Joost van der Westhuizen admits in his autobiography that he's the guy with the holey underpants caught on a sex video snorting drugs

3 November 2009

5 November 2009   Ahead of the award ceremony, Obama marks the first anniversary of his election

5 November 2009 — Party stunted by leadership malaise and resignations

Zuma's World Aids Day pledge to strengthen the roll-out of antiretrovirals comes a decade after Mbeki's denialist dismissal of ARVs as toxic

10 November 2009   Celebrations mark the fall of the infamous barrier twenty years ago

The UN is debating its report, headed by former SA judge Richard Goldstone, which accuses Israel of war crimes in its recent bombardment of Gaza

Board of power parastatal slates CEO Jacob Maroga. He quits but government won't accept his resignation so Chairman Bobby Godsell quits. Public Enterprises Minister Barbara Hogan then backs Godsell but now Maroga wants his job back.

19 November 2009

12 November 2009 Eskom isn't the only parastatal left leaderless due to heads rolling

15 November 2009

Police ministry denies the link between their 'shoot to kill' call and the recent spate of civilian deaths at police hands

Squabbling between Police Minister Nathi Mthethwa and Deputy Fikile Mbalula who is younger but has a higher ANC ranking

22 November 2009

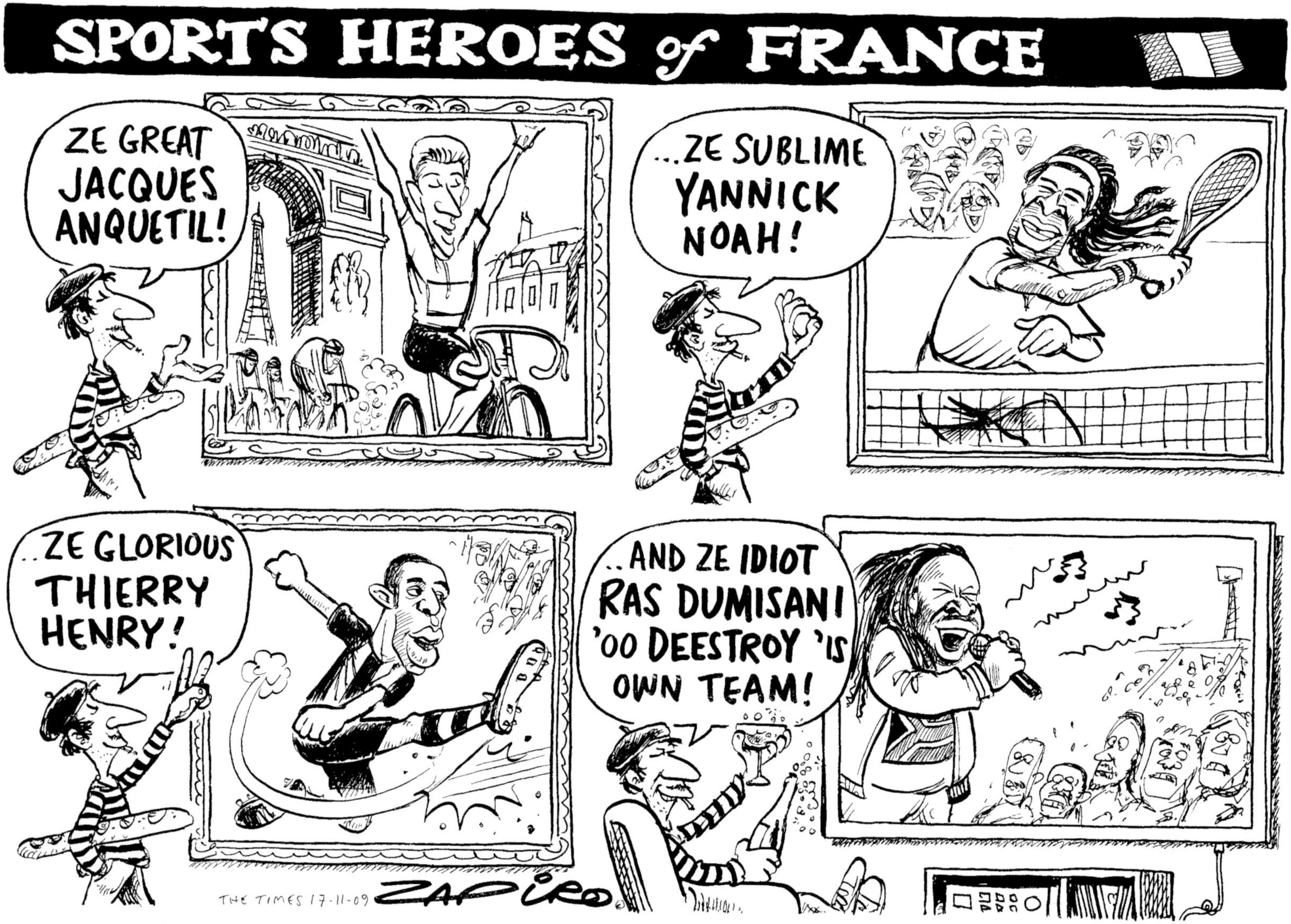
SPORTS HEROES of FRANCE
ZE GREAT JACQUES ANQUETIL!
...ZE SUBLIME YANNICK NOAH!
..ZE GLORIOUS THIERRY HENRY!
..AND ZE IDIOT RAS DUMISANI 'OO DEESTROY 'IS OWN TEAM!
THE TIMES 17-11-09 ZAPIRO

17 November 2009

Springboks lose to France in Toulouse after Durban-born reggae singer Ras Dumisani's hideous butchering of the SA national anthem

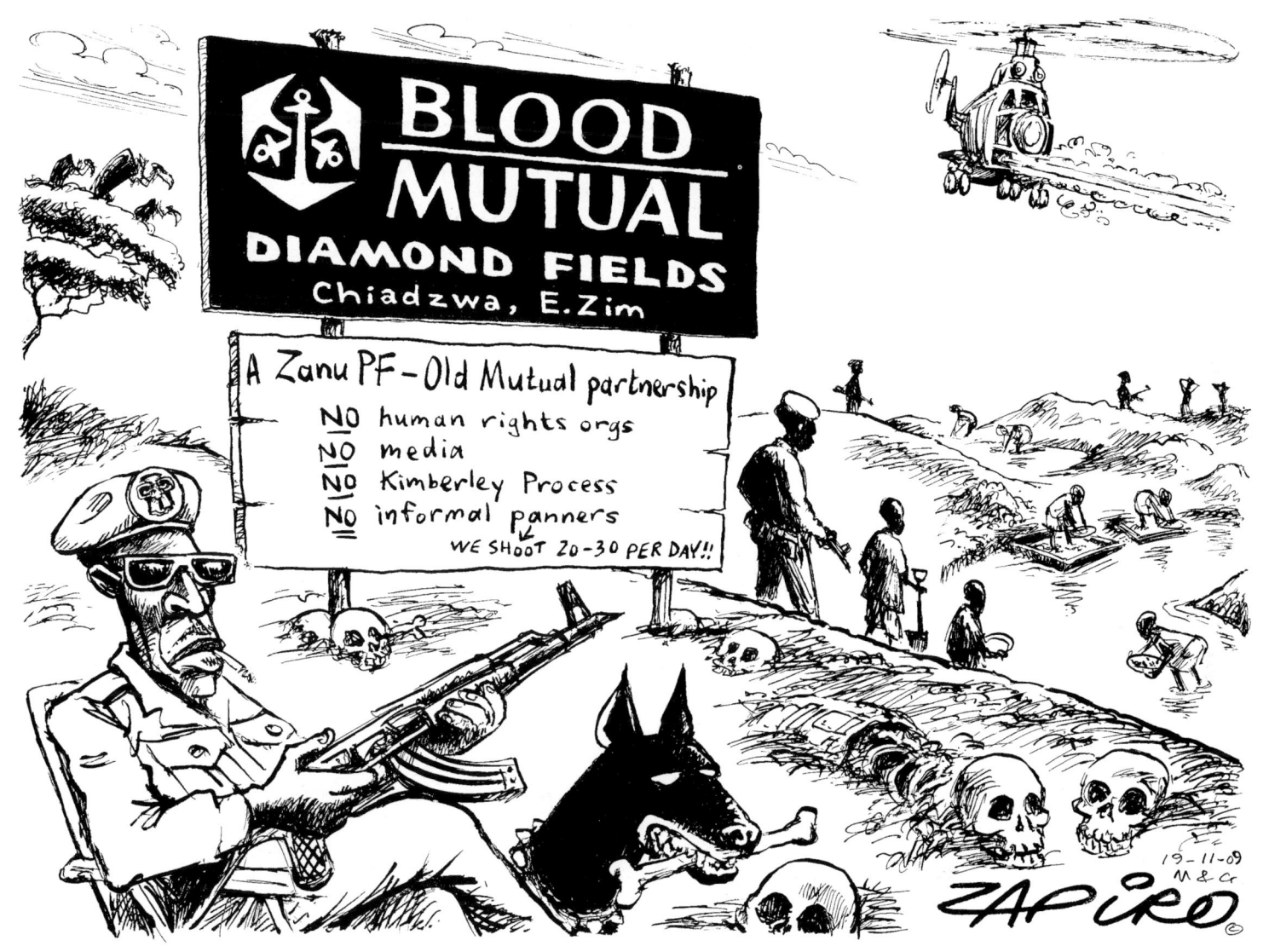

Old Mutual's blood diamonds: company's stake revealed in Zimbabwean minefields notorious for daily police and army atrocities

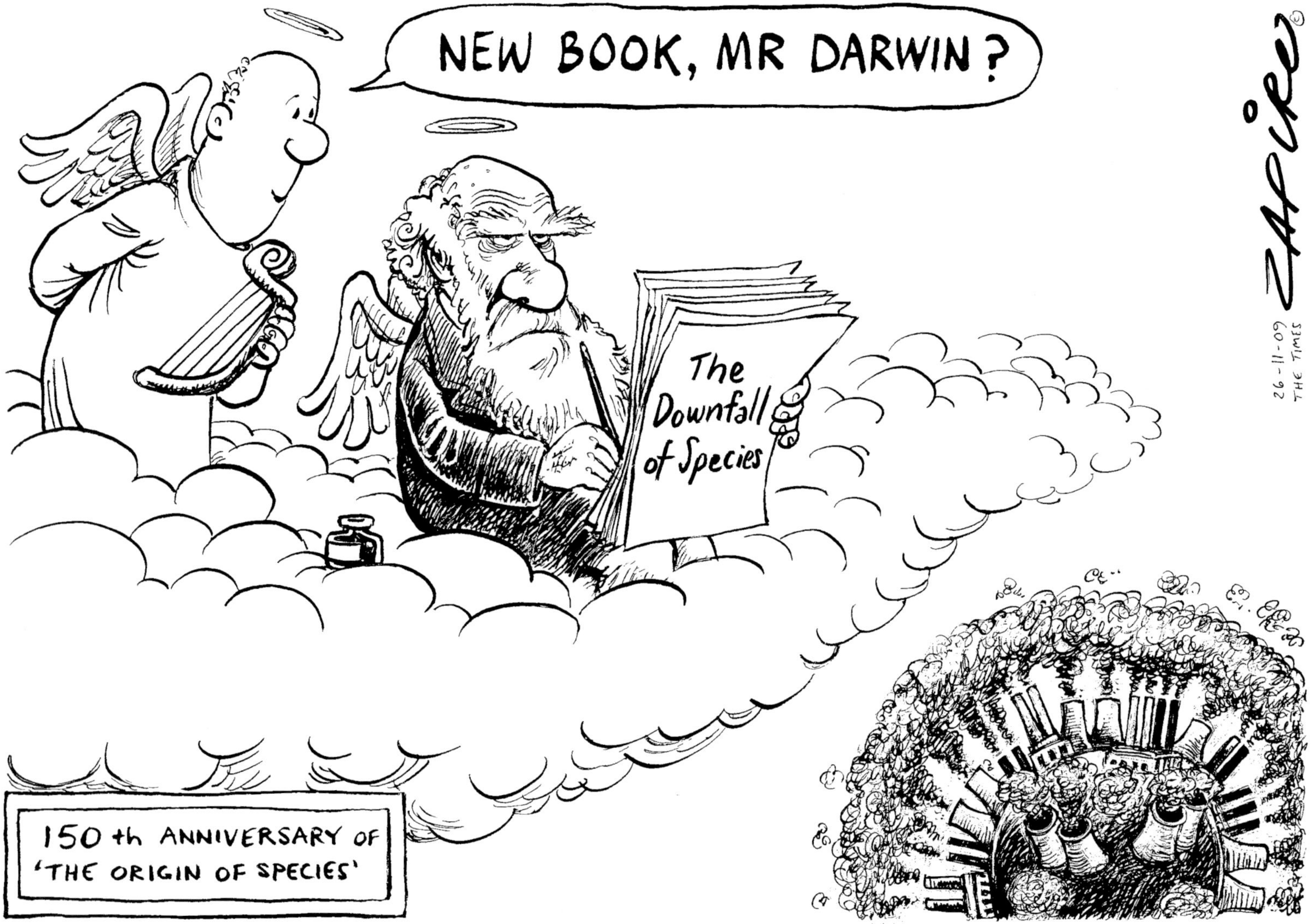
NEW BOOK, MR DARWIN?
The Downfall of Species
150th ANNIVERSARY OF 'THE ORIGIN OF SPECIES'
26-11-09 THE TIMES

26 November 2009

He played this card in the Caster Semenya case and the Eskom management crisis. Now he labels communist leader Jeremy Cronin a 'white messiah' for questioning his call to nationalise mines.

24 November 2009

New Director of the National Prosecuting Authority is the man found by an inquiry to be a liar who unlawfully engineered the axing of then NPA head Vusi Pikoli, who was prosecuting Zuma

26 November 2009

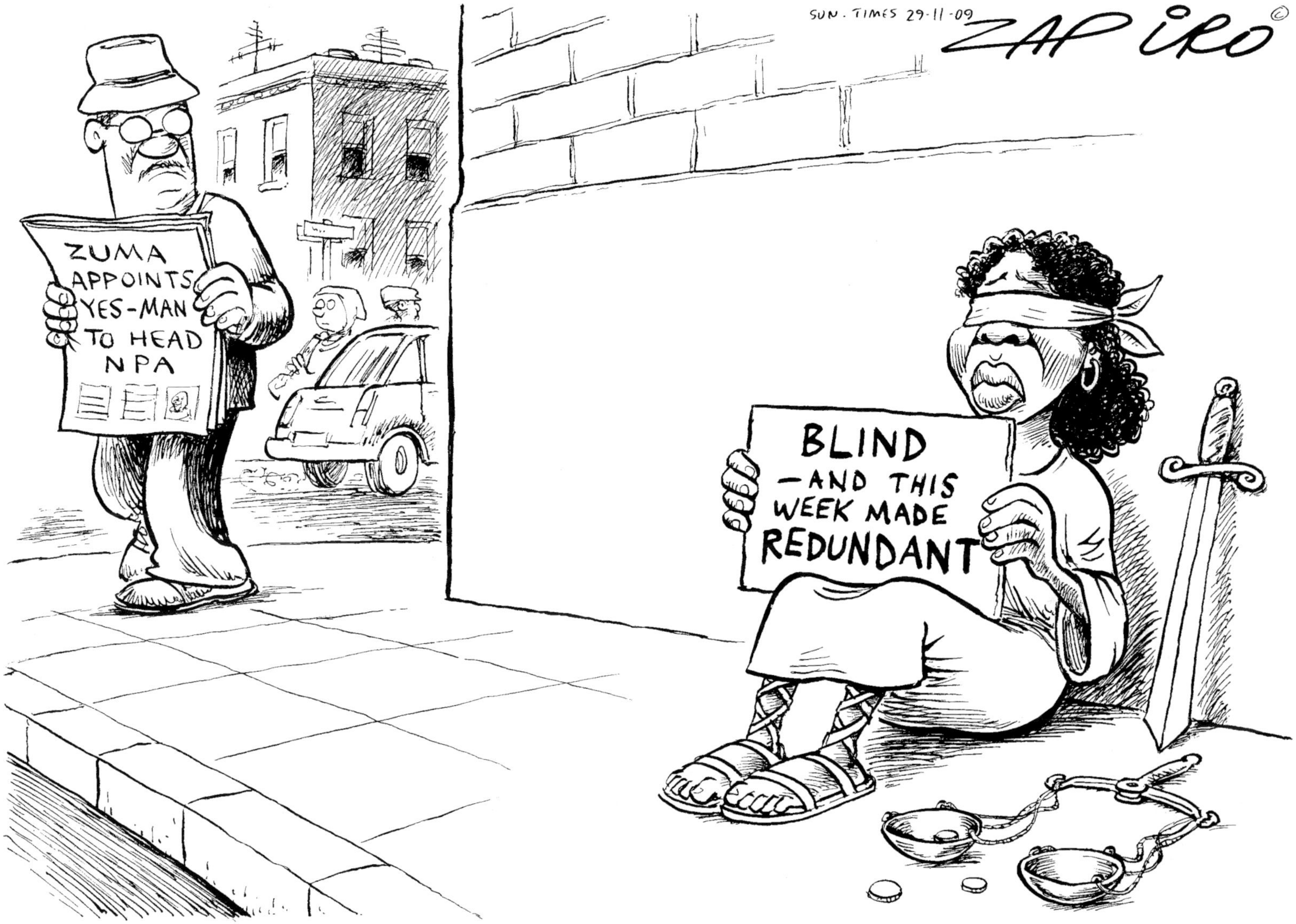
SUN. TIMES 29-11-09
ZAPIRO ©
ZUMA APPOINTS YES-MAN TO HEAD NPA
BLIND
—AND THIS WEEK MADE
REDUNDANT

29 November 2009

1 December 2009

Animal rights activists mount a court challenge against the Zulu Ukweshwama ritual where dozens of bare-handed young men suffocate and mutilate a bull to death

Fifa agrees to consider including Ireland who didn't qualify for the World Cup because of a French goal aided by Thierry Henry's deliberate handball

3 December 2009 — Six months till kick-off

6 December 2009 Fifa ranks us a lowly 86, a record for a World Cup host nation

9 December 2009 — After Tiger Woods crashes into a tree outside his home at 2.25am while fleeing his furious wife Elin, the number of his known affairs multiplies daily (eventual tally is about 18)

SA Airlink plane crash-lands at George Airport and veers onto a highway – the airline's fifth recent serious incident

10 December 2009

Former health minister Manto Tshabalala-Msimang dies of liver disease aged 69. Her disastrous HIV/Aids policies cost 350 000 lives.

Awkwardly timed award ceremony in Oslo, a week after he ordered a major escalation of the war in Afghanistan

Developing nations at the UN Climate Summit in Copenhagen are angry that the Kyoto Protocol – the only mechanism binding rich countries to reduce greenhouse gases – may be scrapped

17 December 2009

10 December 2009 — Talks stall. An effective Copenhagen protocol seems distant.

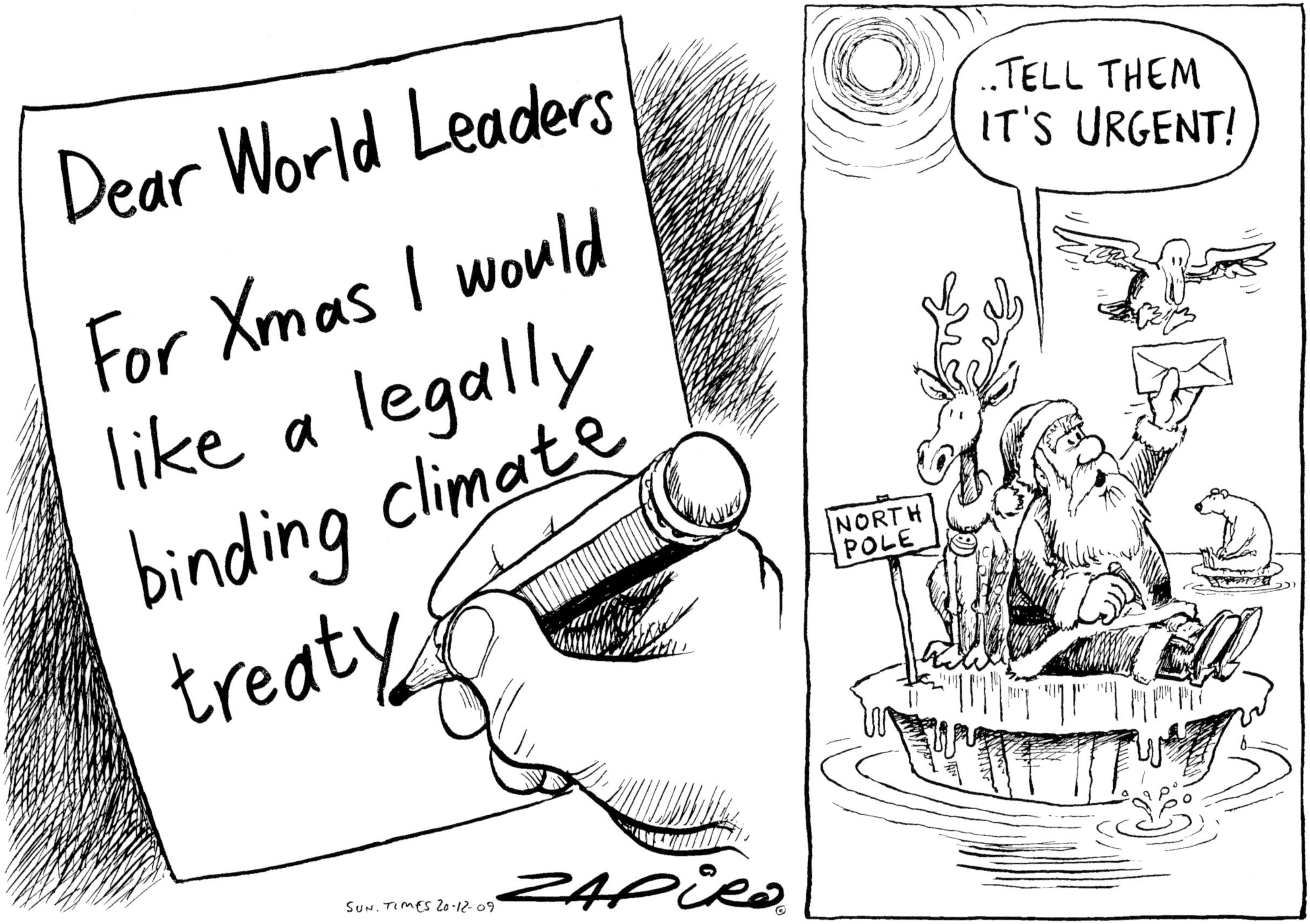
Dear World Leaders
For Xmas I would like a legally binding climate treaty
..TELL THEM IT'S URGENT!
NORTH POLE
SUN. TIMES 20-12-09
ZAPIRO

20 December 2009

Booed at SACP conference and tongue-lashed by Blade Nzimande for being a politically immature right-winger dressed up as a radical, Malema asks Zuma to boycott the conference

15 December 2009

27 December 2009

Ordered by Zuma to cool it, Malema launches offensive to oust the SACP from the Tripartite Alliance

17 January 2010 — Already beset with problems, Haiti is devastated by a 7.0 earthquake which kills at least 230 000

14 January 2010 — After Zuma's secret meeting with jailed apartheid assassin Eugene de Kock, word is he'll pardon De Kock to deflect criticism when he pardons his crony, fraudster Schabir Shaik

19 January 2010 — Fears of party implosion as the Youth League plots to weaken senior leftists

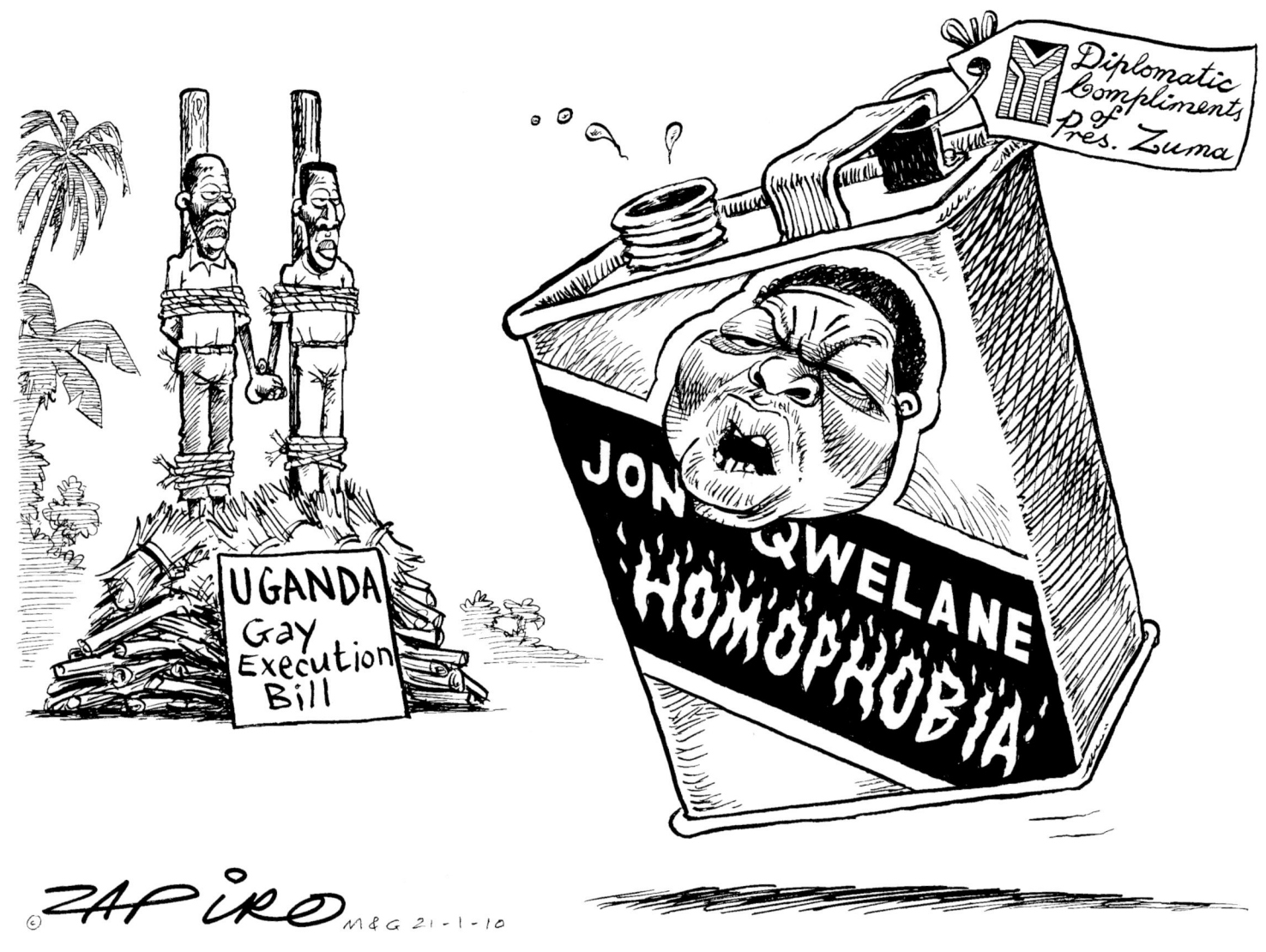

21 January 2010 Anti-gay (but pro-Zuma) columnist to be SA ambassador in the country that aims to kill gays

26 January 2010 — Axed Eskom CEO Jacob Maroga sues for huge payout, unless he's reinstated

24 January 2010

One year in office, hope stalled

12 January 2010

British tabloids lead knee-jerk questioning of South Africa's ability to host a safe World Cup after terrorists kill three people during the Africa Cup of Nations in Angola

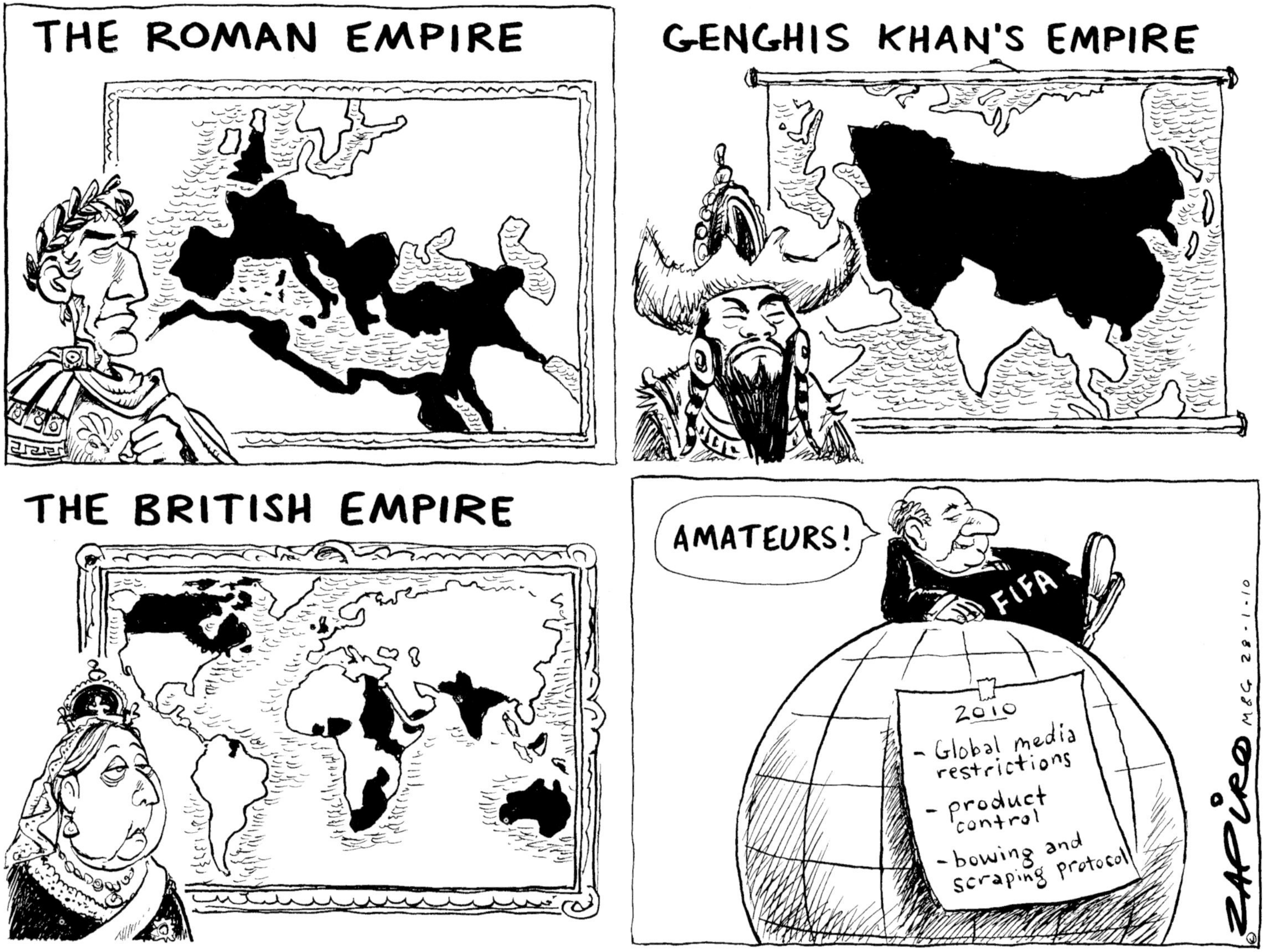
THE ROMAN EMPIRE
GENGHIS KHAN'S EMPIRE
THE BRITISH EMPIRE
AMATEURS!
FIFA
2010
- Global media restrictions
- product control
- bowing and scraping protocol
ZAPIRO
M&G 28·1·10

28 January 2010

2 February 2010

Headline story: Zuma fathered child with daughter of soccer boss Irvin Khoza – more unprotected sex outside his three marriages. And not what he preached on World Aids Day.

4 February 2010   Twenty offspring and counting. Spin-doctors say he's engaged to his love-child's mom.

4 February 2010 — Two decades since De Klerk's February 2 speech announcing Mandela's release

Ahead of key address
(Artist's note: the shower has been suspended since his inauguration)

9 February 2010 — Angered that he broke a promise to them to behave, party leaders make him apologise

11 February 2010 — Anniversary of prison release

14 February 2010 — Reports of yet more offspring numbering up to 34

16 February 2010 — State of the Nation address

18 February 2010 — Ahead of Finance Minister Pravin Gordhan's first budget

18 February 2010 — Iconic London studio to be sold off as home technology shrinks the music industry

21 February 2010

As he trumpets nationalisation, the media reveal the extent of his assets – paid for in cash – and the many state tenders he's secured

This rather unspecific plot revealed at press conference as crisis-hit Eskom announces huge price hike

Not for the first time, Zuma talks up Malema's 'leadership qualities'

Accused of giving the finger to the president's blue-light convoy,
UCT student Chumani Maxwele is arrested at gunpoint and roughed up

4 March 2010

About to launch a women's photo exhibition, the minister sees the photos and denounces them as 'immoral pornography'

4 March 2010 — Stadiums are almost ready. The promised community upgrades are another story.

Budget airline Kulula forced to pull its World Cup spoof advert which Fifa calls a trademark infringement

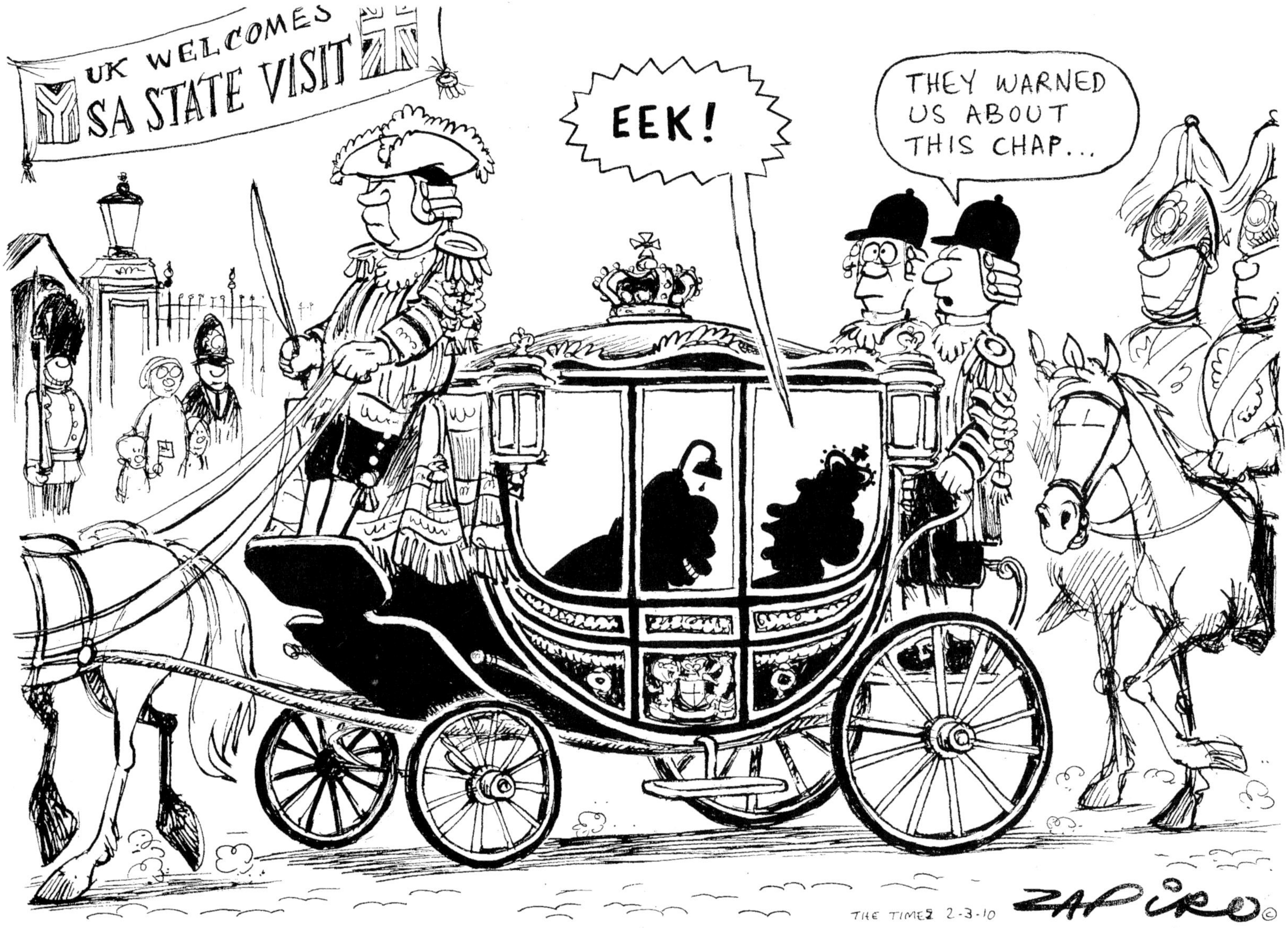
UK WELCOMES
SA STATE VISIT
EEK!
THEY WARNED US ABOUT THIS CHAP...
THE TIMES 2-3-10
ZAPIRO ©

2 March 2010

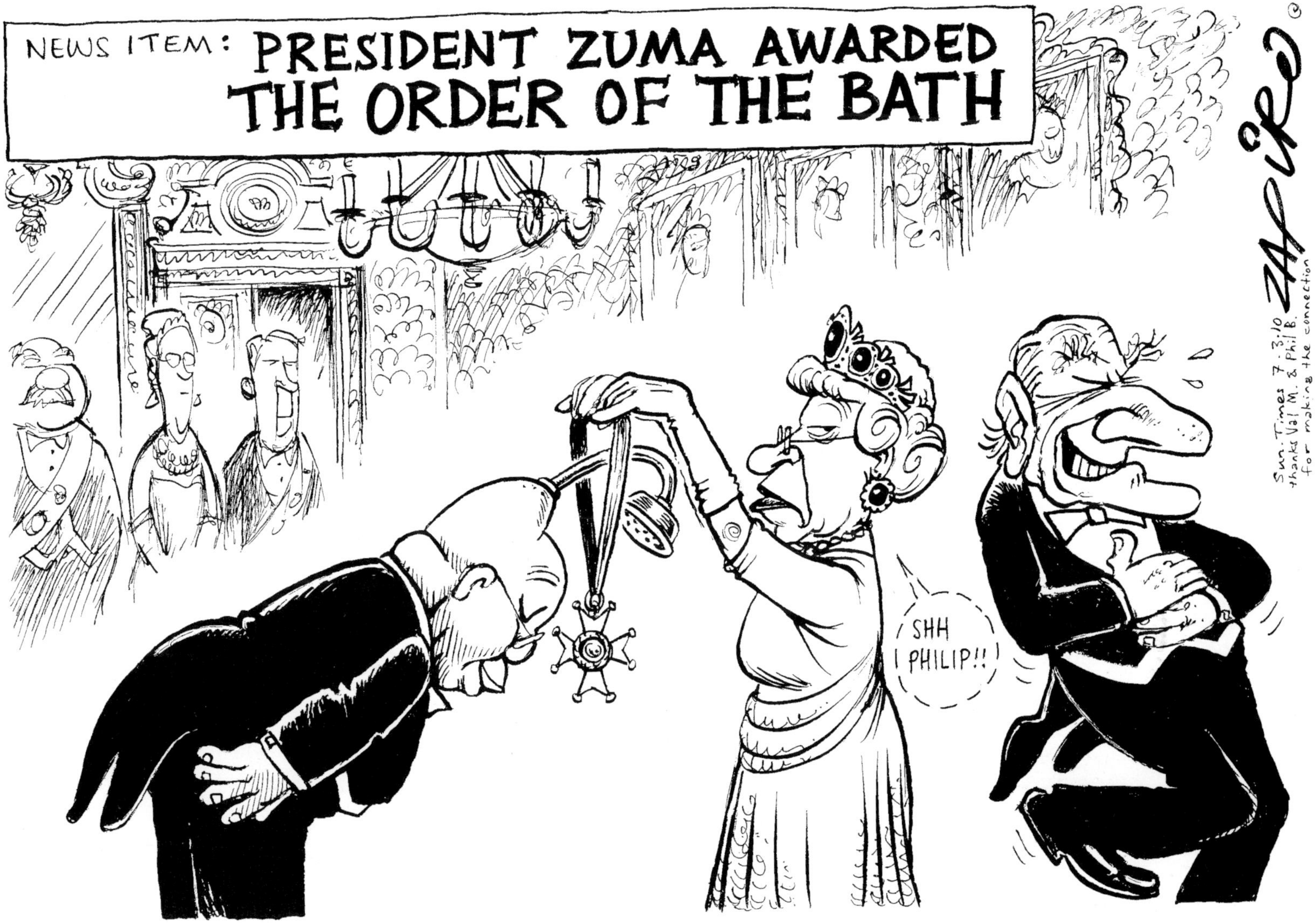
NEWS ITEM: PRESIDENT ZUMA AWARDED THE ORDER OF THE BATH
SHH PHILIP!!
Sun. Times 7.3.10
thanks Val M. & Phil B. for making the connection

7 March 2010

11 March 2010

Mauled by UK media and now home to fresh crisis: ten months in office and he's failed to declare his assets

Equality Court upholds gender group's complaint against him for saying Zuma's rape accuser enjoyed having sex

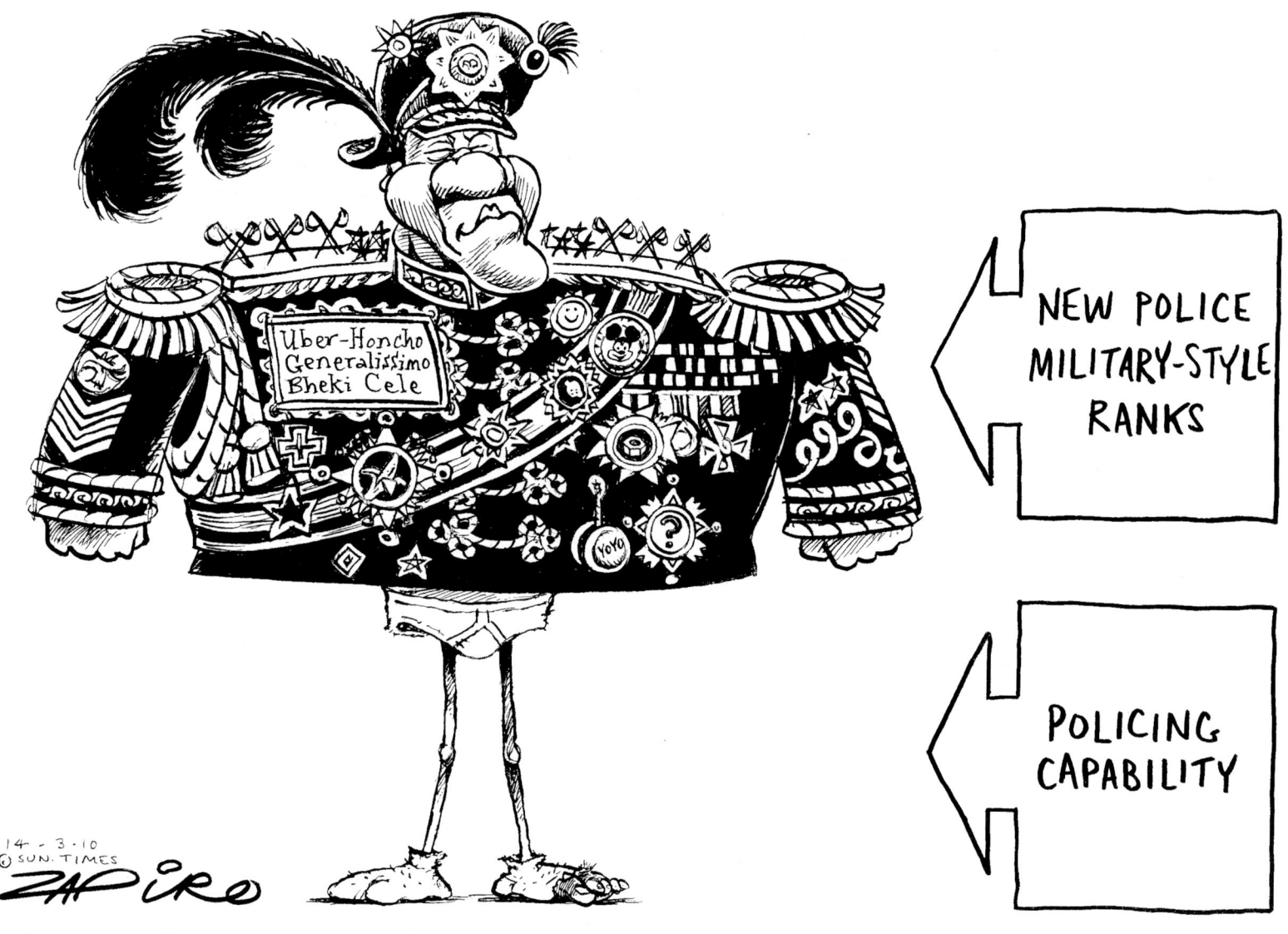

14 March 2010 — Police militarised. National Commissioner insists he be addressed as 'general'.

18 March 2010 Israel scuppers planned US-brokered peace talks by announcing a 1600-house Jewish settlement

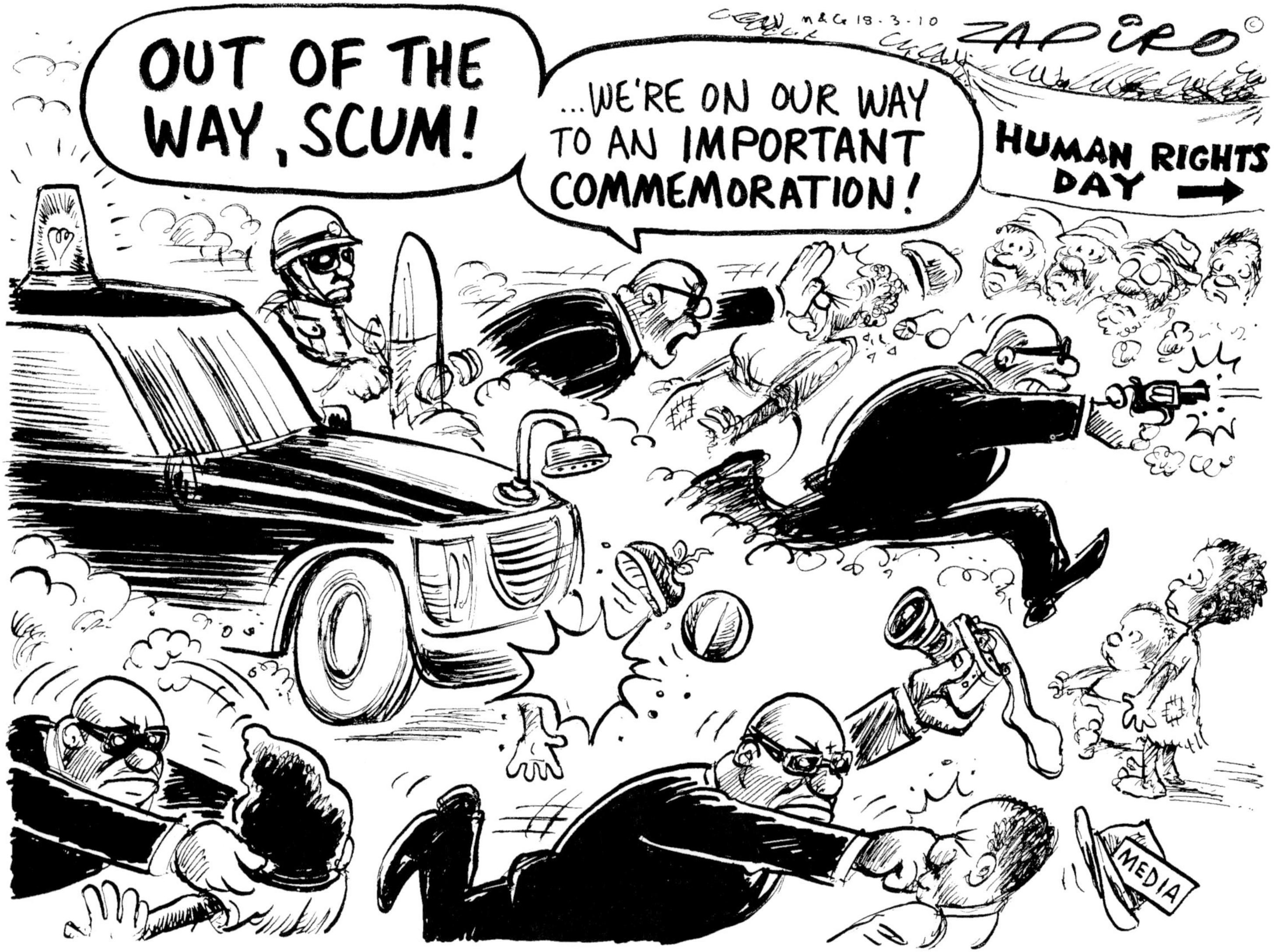
OUT OF THE WAY, SCUM!
...WE'RE ON OUR WAY TO AN IMPORTANT COMMEMORATION!
HUMAN RIGHTS DAY
ZAPIRO
M&G 18-3-10
MEDIA

18 March 2010

Calls to rein in 'Zuma's blue-light bullies' after separate assaults on a grandmother and a photographer

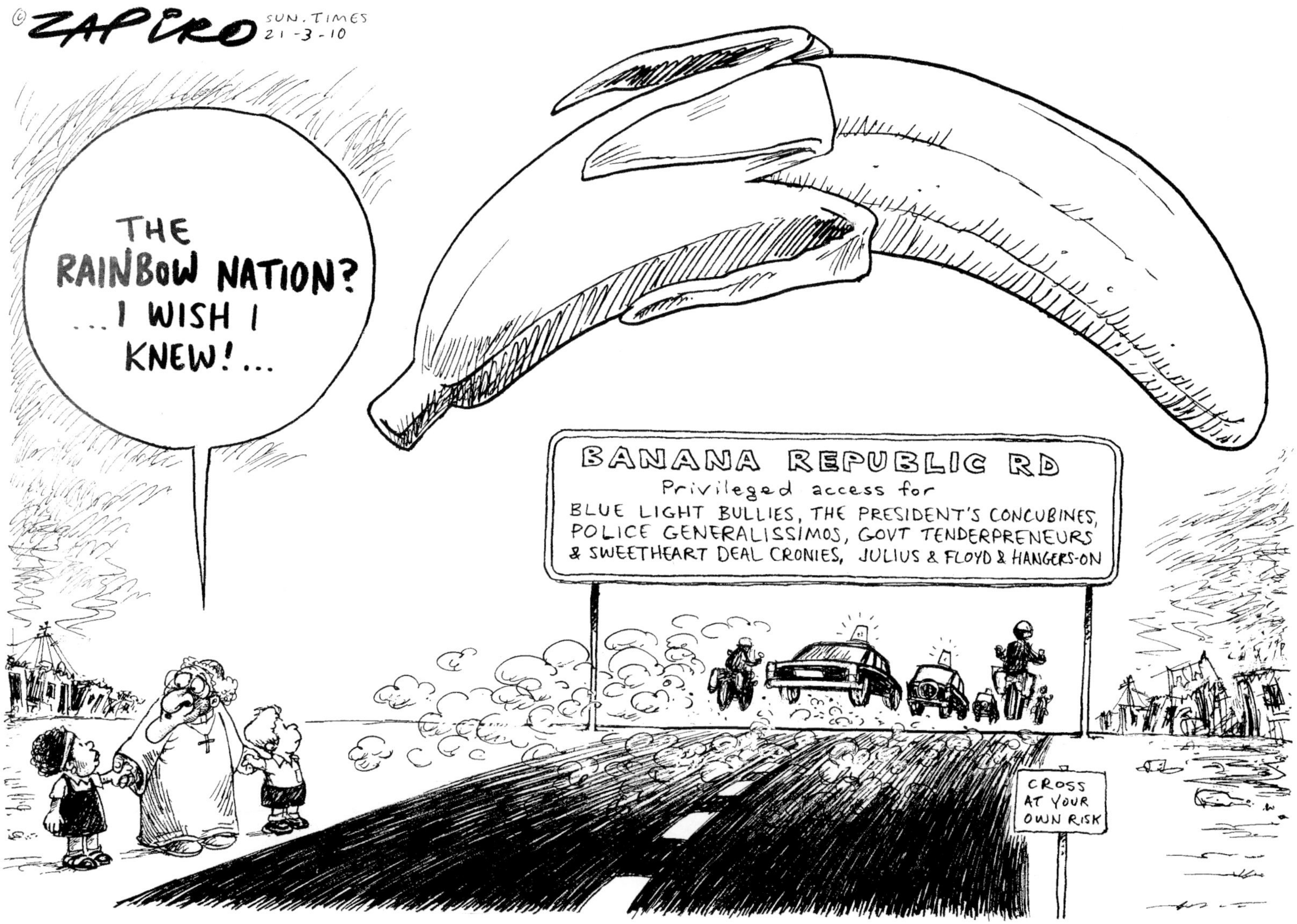
© ZAPIRO SUN. TIMES 21-3-10
THE RAINBOW NATION? ...I WISH I KNEW!...
BANANA REPUBLIC RD
Privileged access for
BLUE LIGHT BULLIES, THE PRESIDENT'S CONCUBINES, POLICE GENERALISSIMOS, GOVT TENDERPRENEURS & SWEETHEART DEAL CRONIES, JULIUS & FLOYD & HANGERS-ON
CROSS AT YOUR OWN RISK

21 March 2010 Human Rights Day

25 March 2010 — Four opposition parties pledge to form a joint front

Paedophile priests crisis. Benedict XVI pressured to apologise but it seems he protected abusers before becoming pope.

25 March 2010

1 April 2010 — At Easter he blames the media for a smear campaign

4 April 2010

A week after Zuma claimed progress on power-sharing, bickering leaders take time out to condemn homosexuality

1 April 2010

Singing this old struggle song in 2010 is provocative but Judge Halgryn's ruling goes too far. Malema also provokes the PAC by writing them out of the 1960 Sharpeville uprising.

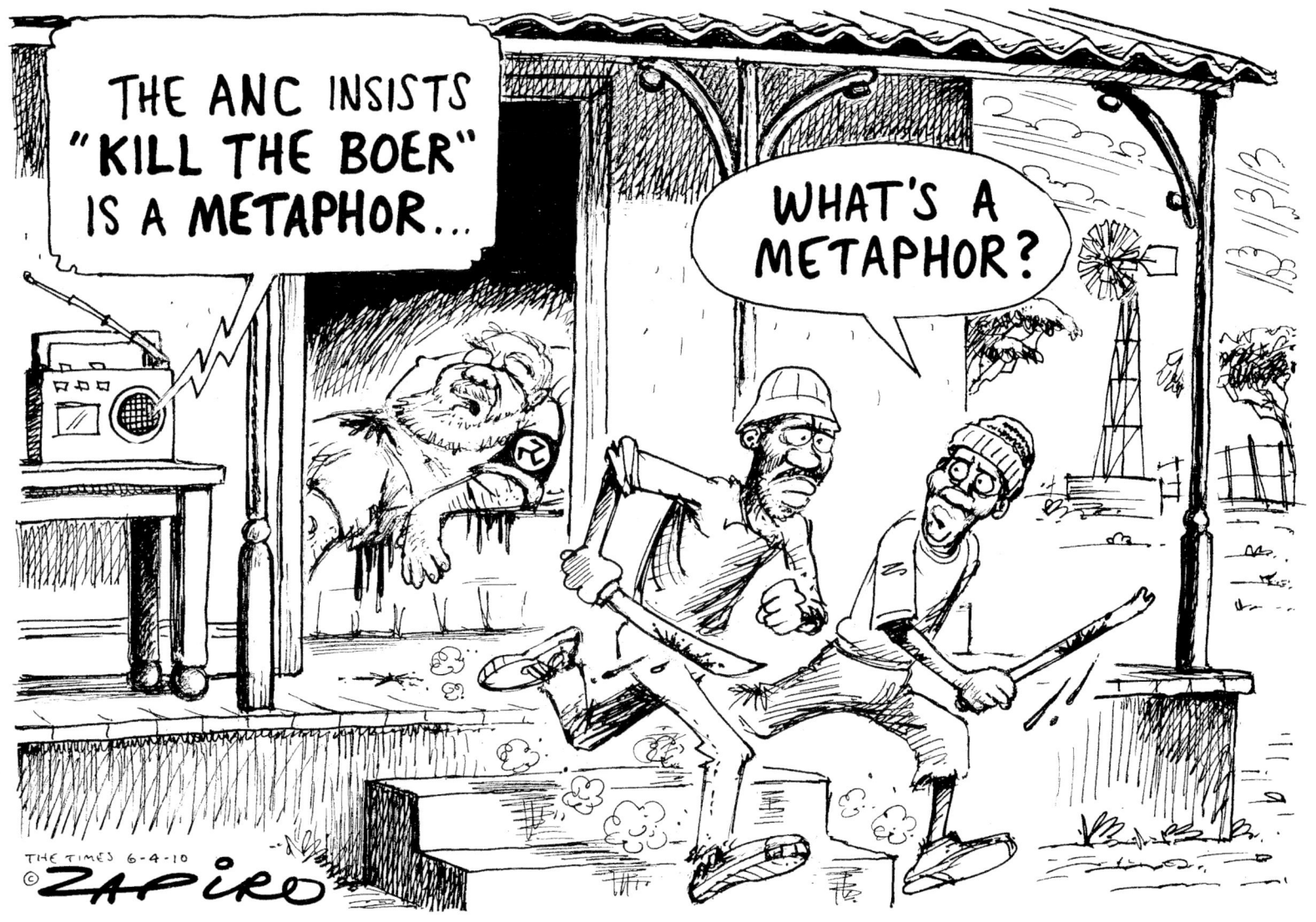

6 March 2010

AWB leader Eugene TerreBlanche hacked to death with a panga on his farm near Ventersdorp. Two farmworkers arrested.

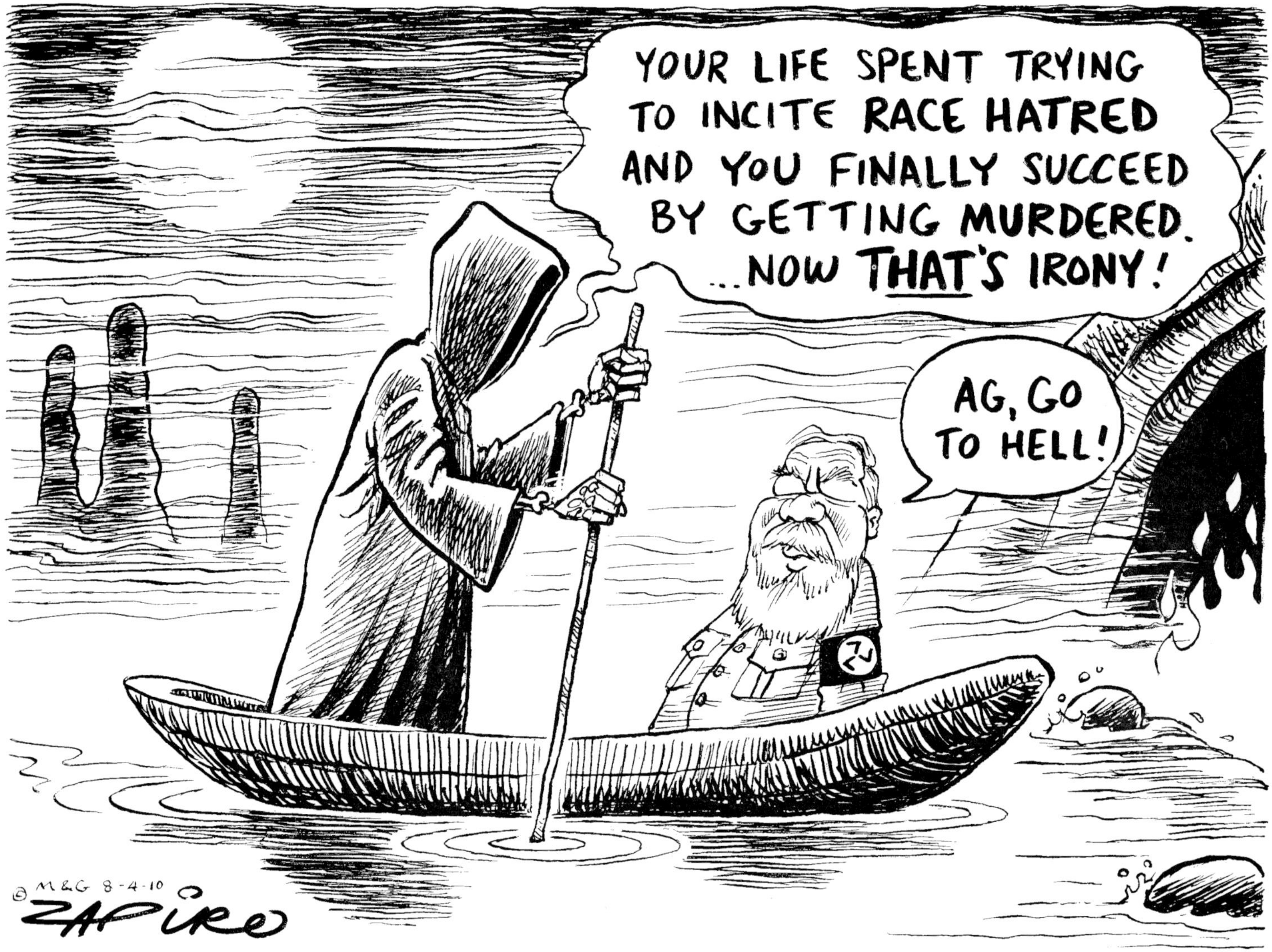
YOUR LIFE SPENT TRYING TO INCITE RACE HATRED AND YOU FINALLY SUCCEED BY GETTING MURDERED. ...NOW THAT'S IRONY!
AG, GO TO HELL!
© M&G 8-4-10
ZAPIRO

8 April 2010

He was found with his pants down. Killed over a pay dispute?
Or was sex involved, as the accused briefly allege? Old rumours surface.

13 April 2010

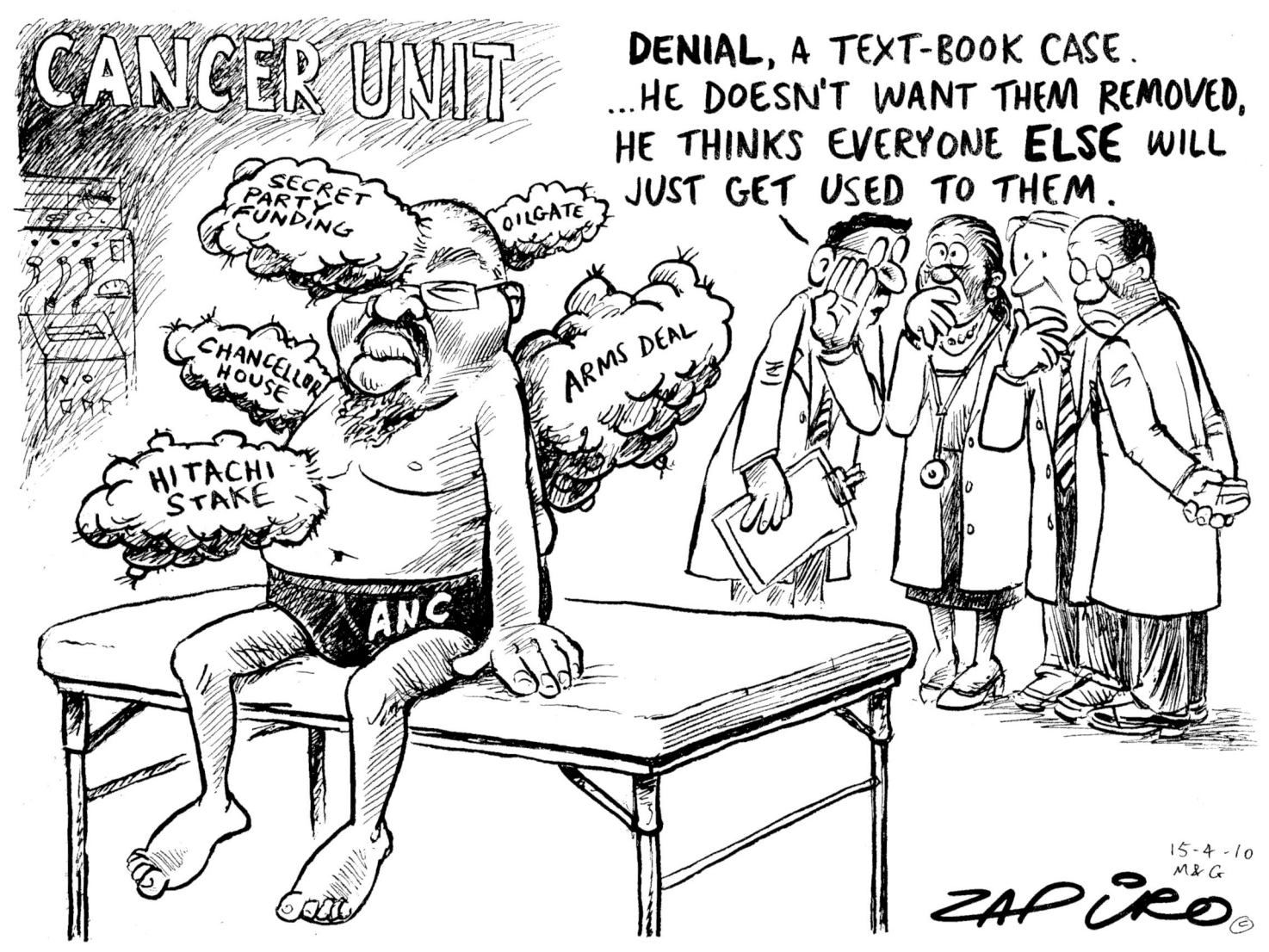

When Hitachi Power gets a R30bn World Bank loan, a cool R1bn will go to the ANC via a subcontract. The ANC sees no conflict of interest (though soon sells its stake).

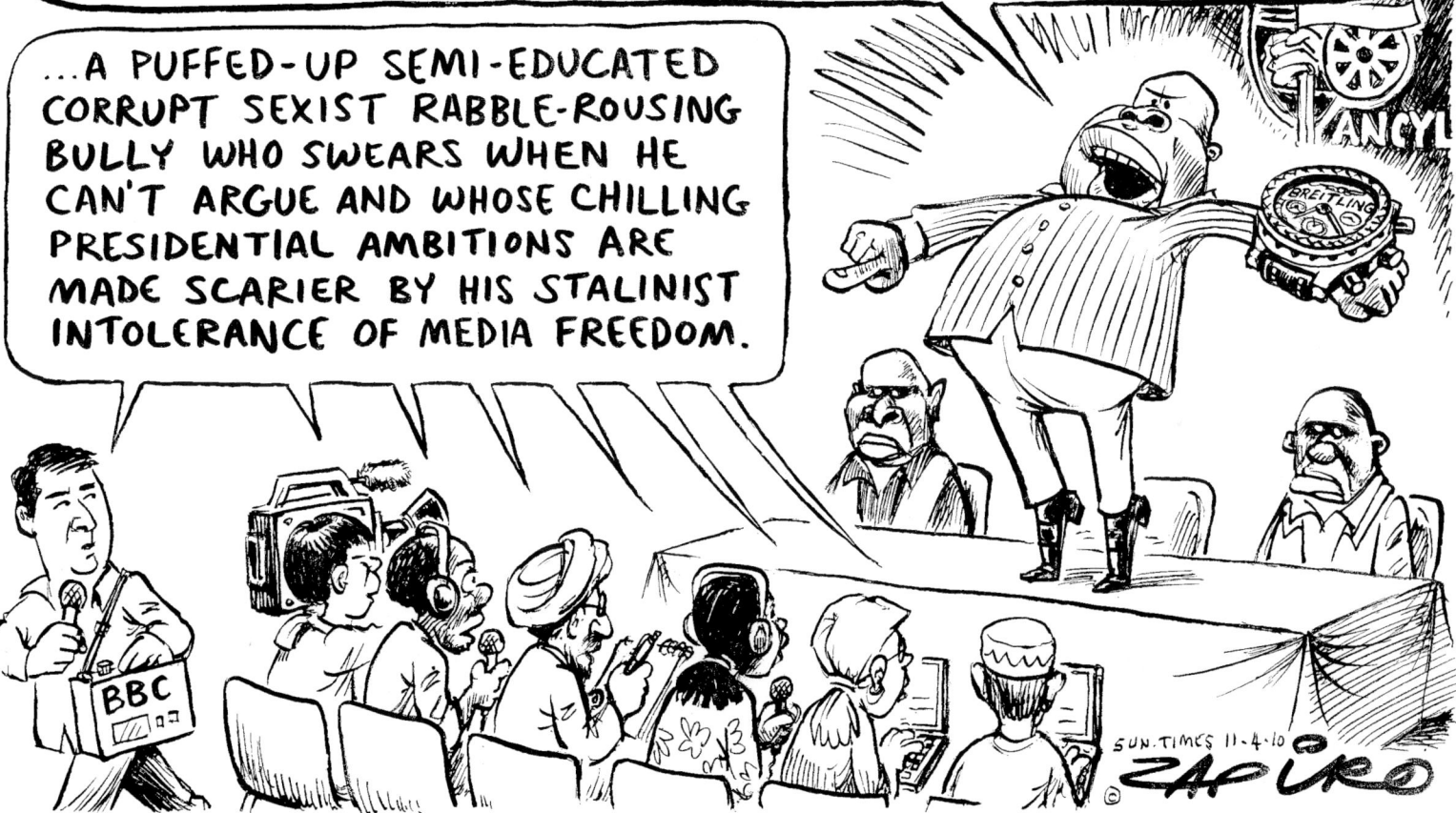

11 April 2010 — Ejecting the BBC's Jonah Fisher and calling him a bastard and a bloody agent

20 April 2010 — Ash cloud from Iceland's volcano halts air traffic across much of Europe

18 April 2010 — Frustration and scuffles as computer crashes mar Fifa's final phase of sales

25 April 2010

The ANC's disciplinary committee is charging Malema for his recent conduct which includes saying Zuma's rebuke of the Youth League makes him worse than Mbeki

22 April 2010 — 30 years of independence

22 April 2010

For criticising Israel in his UN report, Judge Goldstone is banned from his grandson's Barmitzvah. In the end he does attend.

29 April 2010

Corruption trial of ex-police chief Jackie Selebi. His defence: details of bribes totalling R1.2 million from druglord Glenn Agliotti are a media smear.

Branded a liar by the prosecution. Antics include displaying clearly fabricated documents and saying his wife shredded a key document he was about to bring to court.

4 May 2010

Acrimonious meeting ahead of party elections after leader Mosiuoa Lekota accused deputy Mbhazima Shilowa of mismanaging funds. Shilowa faction aims to oust Lekota.

2 May 2010

6 May 2010   Shilowa deemed innocent until proven guilty. Lekota's apology 'accepted'.

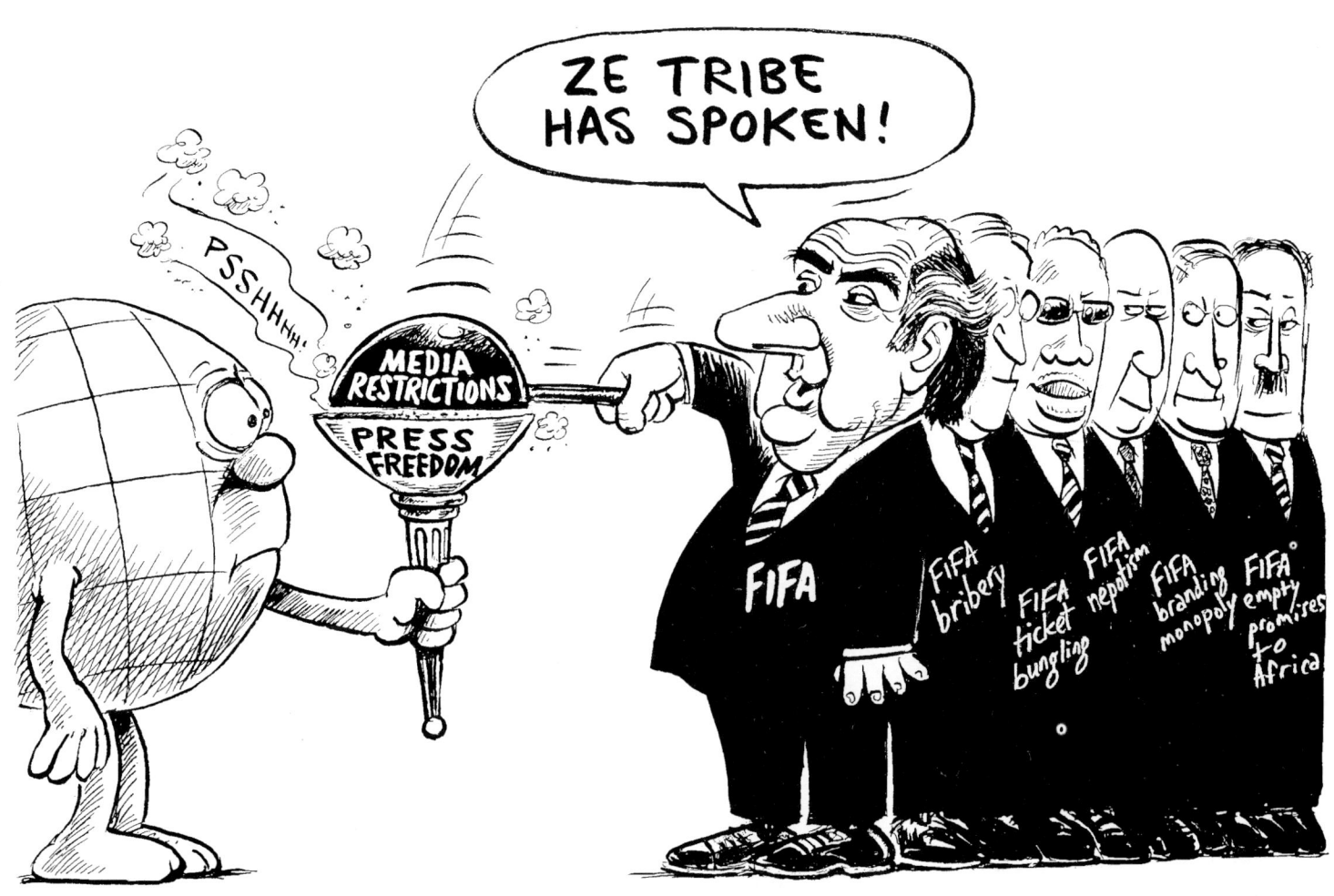

6 May 2010 Obedience demanded. Certain critical journalists barred from Fifa press conferences.

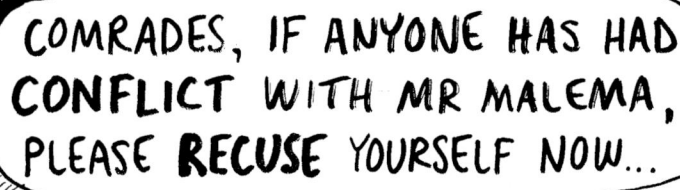

9 May 2010 — Committee chaired by Derek Hanekom. Cabinet ministers Zola Skweyiya, Susan Shabangu and Collins Chabane have had run-ins with Malema. Two recuse themselves. He wants more.

13 May 2010 — Guilty of sowing party disunity, he has to apologise to Zuma and take anger management classes

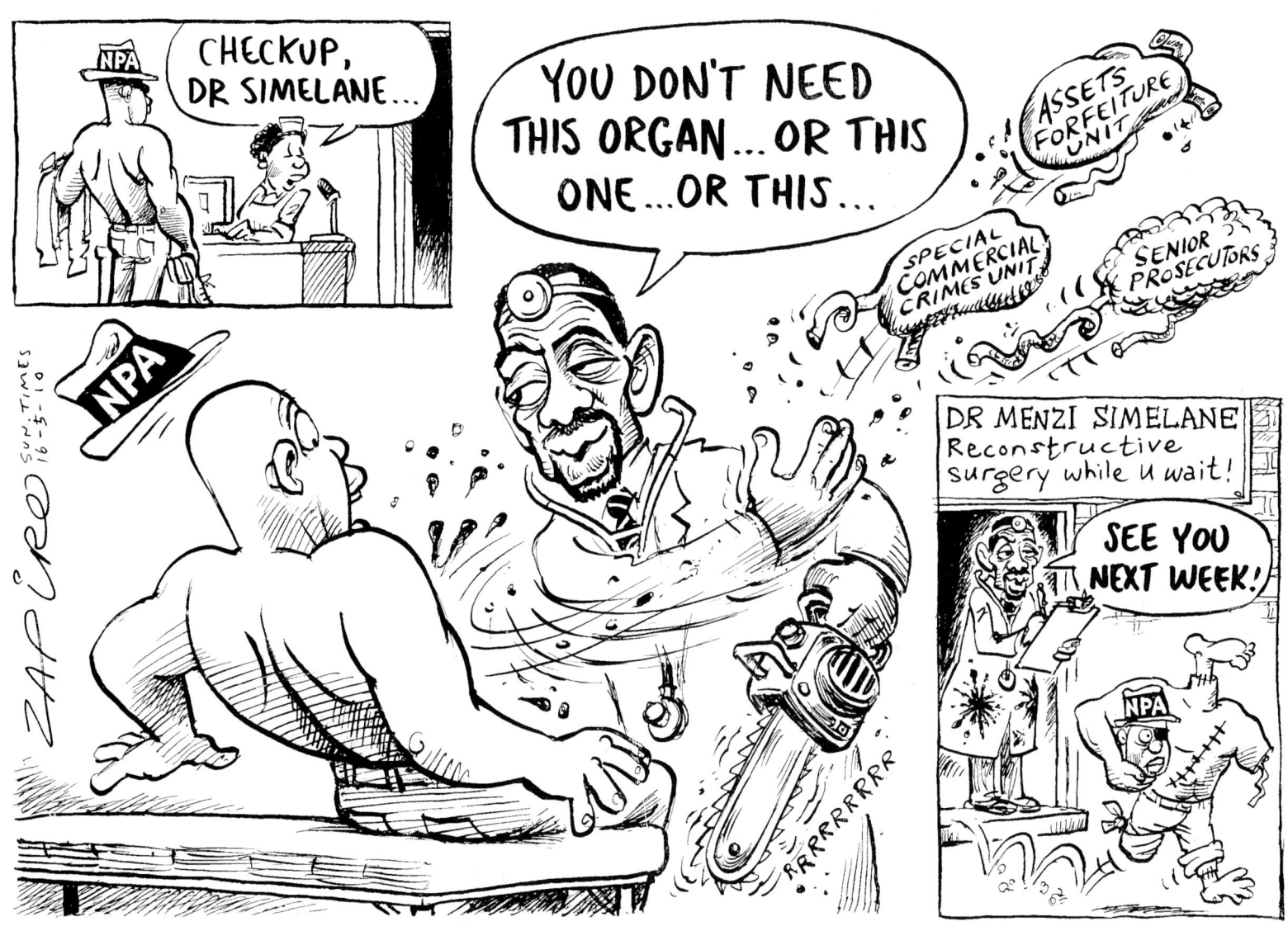

16 May 2010 — 'Restructuring' is what new NPA director calls the gutting of successful units

18 May 2010 — Dr Frederik van Zyl Slabbert dies aged 70

No clarity yet on the overlapping roles of Ebrahim Patel's ministry and the new NPC headed by former finance minister Trevor Manuel

20 May 2010

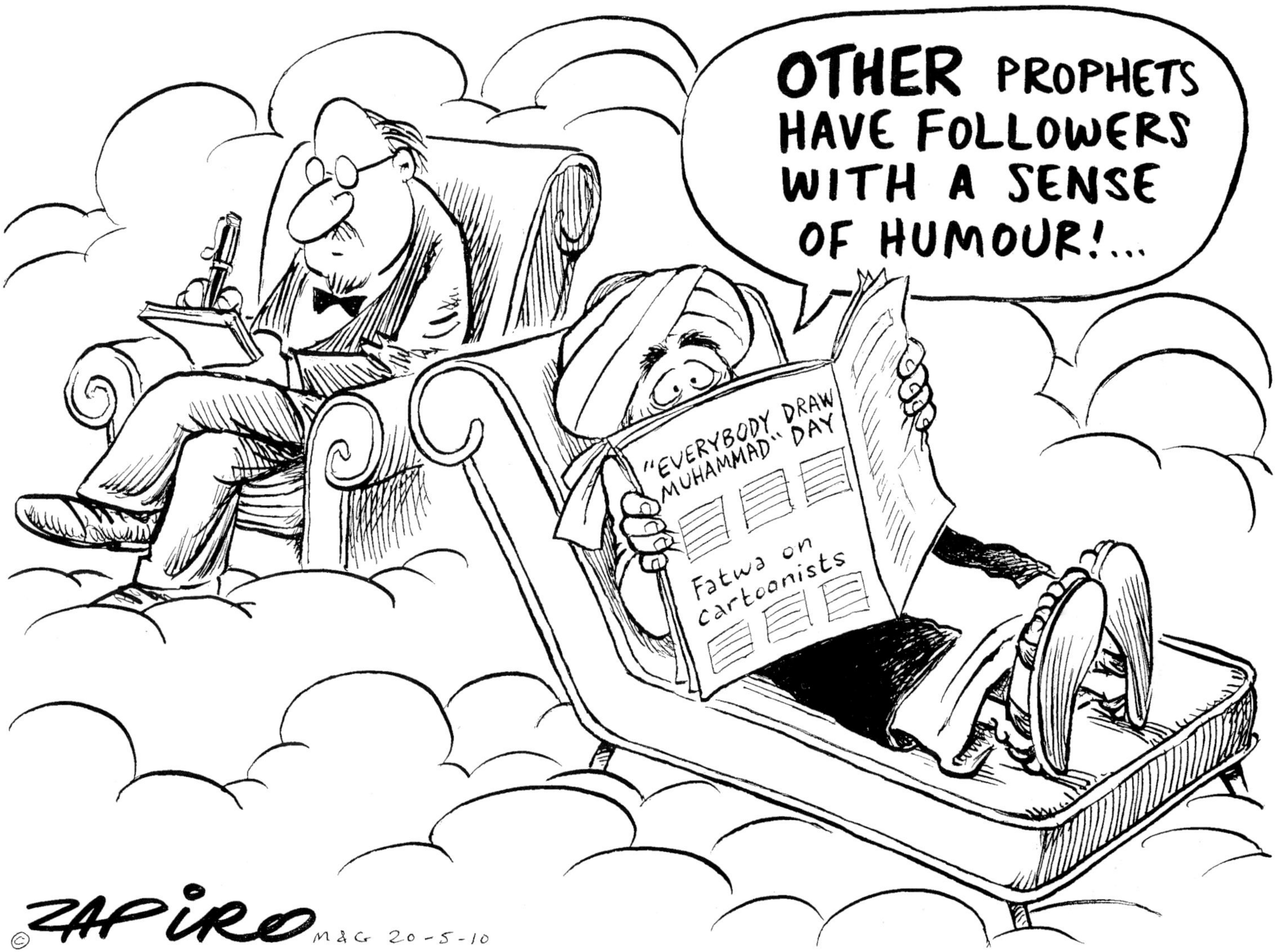
OTHER PROPHETS HAVE FOLLOWERS WITH A SENSE OF HUMOUR!...
"EVERYBODY DRAW MUHAMMAD" DAY
Fatwa on cartoonists
© ZAPIRO M&G 20-5-10

20 May 2010

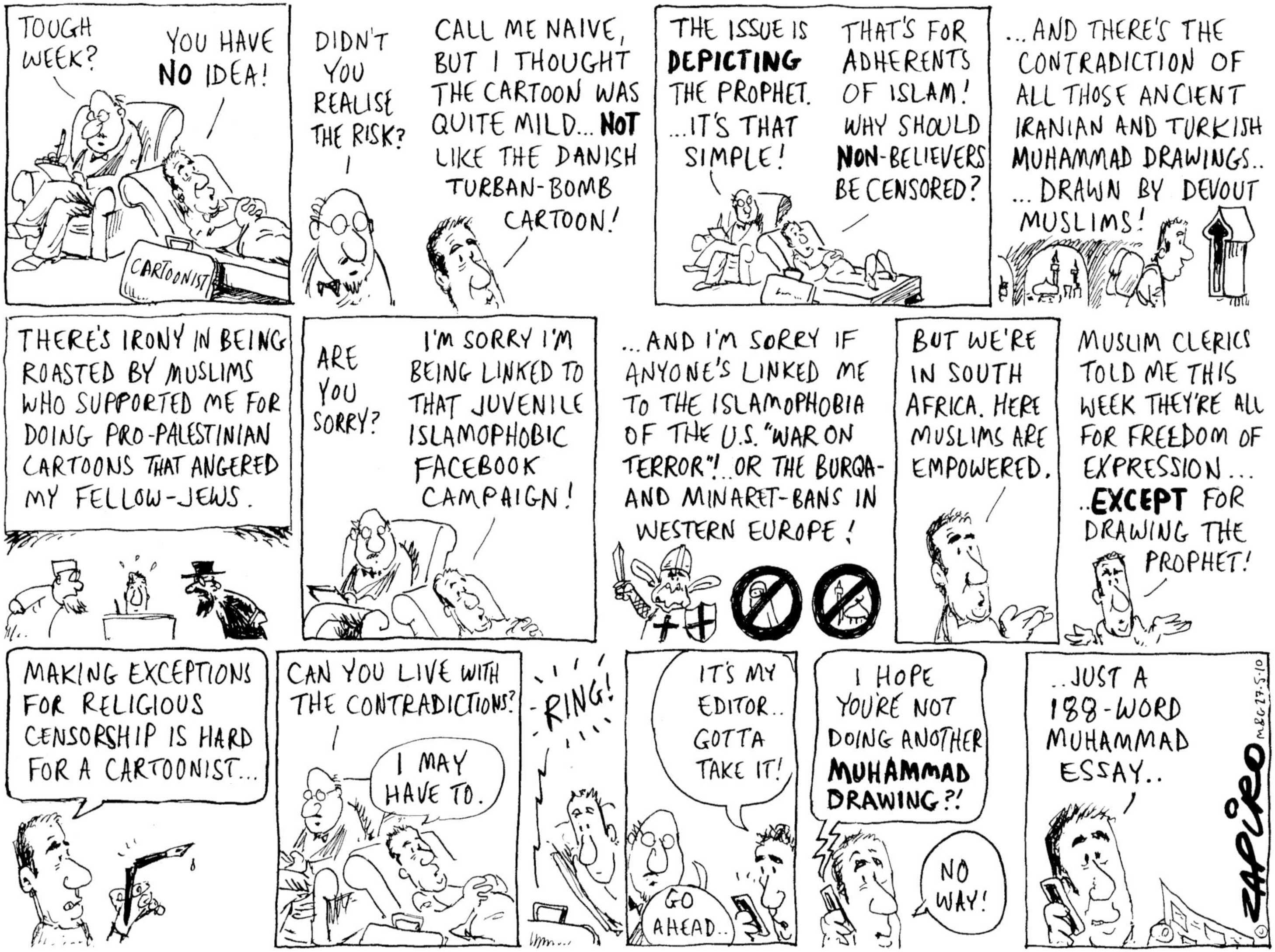
TOUGH WEEK?
YOU HAVE **NO** IDEA!
CARTOONIST
DIDN'T YOU REALISE THE RISK?
CALL ME NAIVE, BUT I THOUGHT THE CARTOON WAS QUITE MILD... **NOT** LIKE THE DANISH TURBAN-BOMB CARTOON!
THE ISSUE IS **DEPICTING** THE PROPHET. ...IT'S THAT SIMPLE!
THAT'S FOR ADHERENTS OF ISLAM! WHY SHOULD **NON**-BELIEVERS BE CENSORED?
...AND THERE'S THE CONTRADICTION OF ALL THOSE ANCIENT IRANIAN AND TURKISH MUHAMMAD DRAWINGS.. ...DRAWN BY DEVOUT MUSLIMS!
THERE'S IRONY IN BEING ROASTED BY MUSLIMS WHO SUPPORTED ME FOR DOING PRO-PALESTINIAN CARTOONS THAT ANGERED MY FELLOW-JEWS.
ARE YOU SORRY?
I'M SORRY I'M BEING LINKED TO THAT JUVENILE ISLAMOPHOBIC FACEBOOK CAMPAIGN!
...AND I'M SORRY IF ANYONE'S LINKED ME TO THE ISLAMOPHOBIA OF THE U.S. "WAR ON TERROR"!..OR THE BURQA- AND MINARET-BANS IN WESTERN EUROPE!
BUT WE'RE IN SOUTH AFRICA. HERE MUSLIMS ARE EMPOWERED.
MUSLIM CLERICS TOLD ME THIS WEEK THEY'RE ALL FOR FREEDOM OF EXPRESSION... ..**EXCEPT** FOR DRAWING THE PROPHET!
MAKING EXCEPTIONS FOR RELIGIOUS CENSORSHIP IS HARD FOR A CARTOONIST...
CAN YOU LIVE WITH THE CONTRADICTIONS?
I MAY HAVE TO.
RING!
IT'S MY EDITOR.. GOTTA TAKE IT!
GO AHEAD..
I HOPE YOU'RE NOT DOING ANOTHER **MUHAMMAD DRAWING**?!
NO WAY!
..JUST A 188-WORD MUHAMMAD ESSAY..
ZAPIRO
M&G 27.5.10

27 May 2010

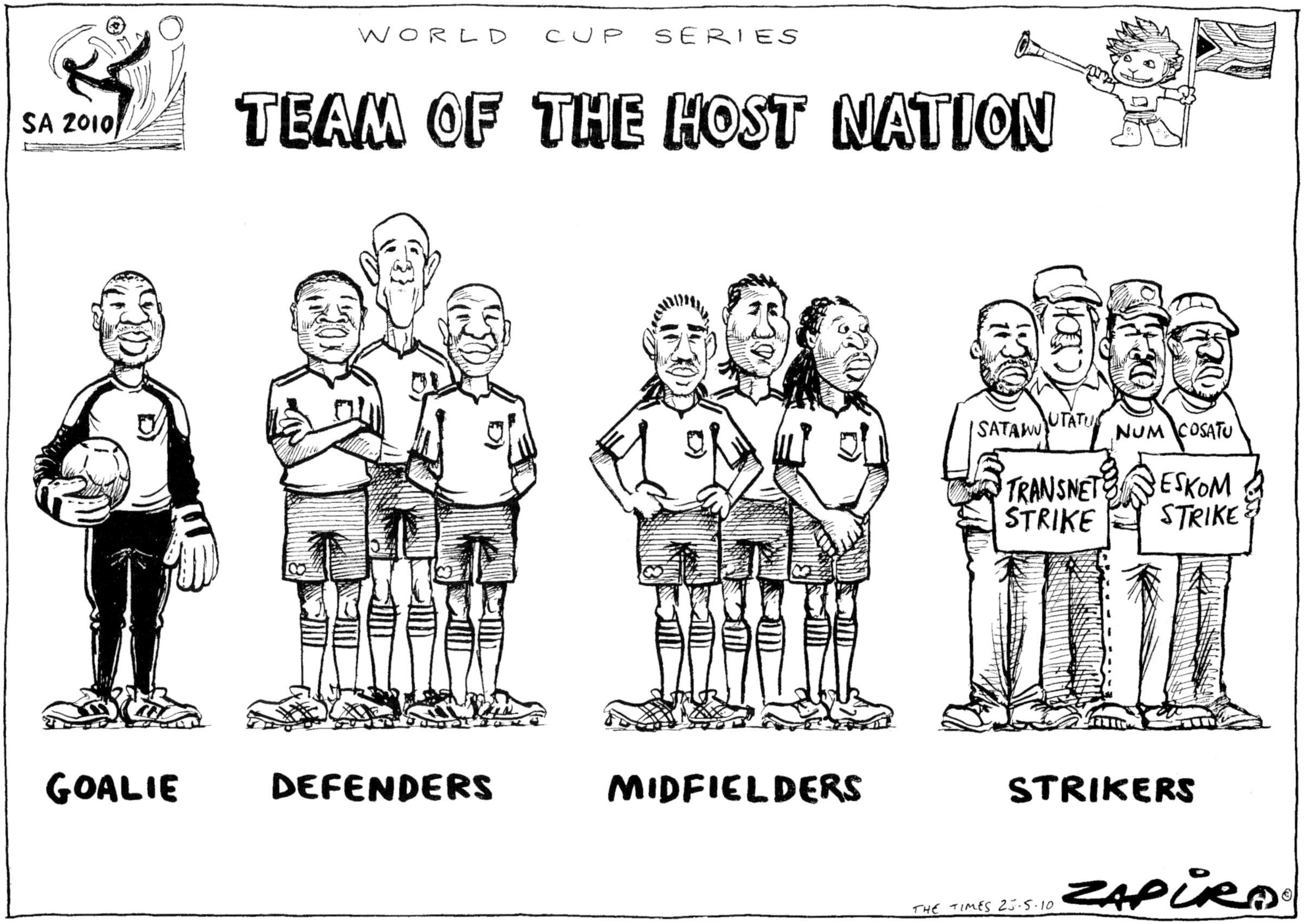
WORLD CUP SERIES
SA 2010
TEAM OF THE HOST NATION
GOALIE
DEFENDERS
MIDFIELDERS
STRIKERS
SATAWU
UTATU
NUM
COSATU
TRANSNET STRIKE
ESKOM STRIKE
THE TIMES 25·5·10
ZAPIRO

25 May 2010

Two weeks till kick-off

27 May 2010 — Malawi gay couple sentenced to 14 years' hard labour and not a peep from our government

Holding elective conference to chart their course,
but factionalism is so vicious that the vote is postponed

1 June 2010

Even Israel's allies join global condemnation of the killing of 10 pro-Palestinian activists when Israeli marines storm a Turkish ship that is part of an aid flotilla trying to breach Israel's blockade of Gaza

3 June 2010

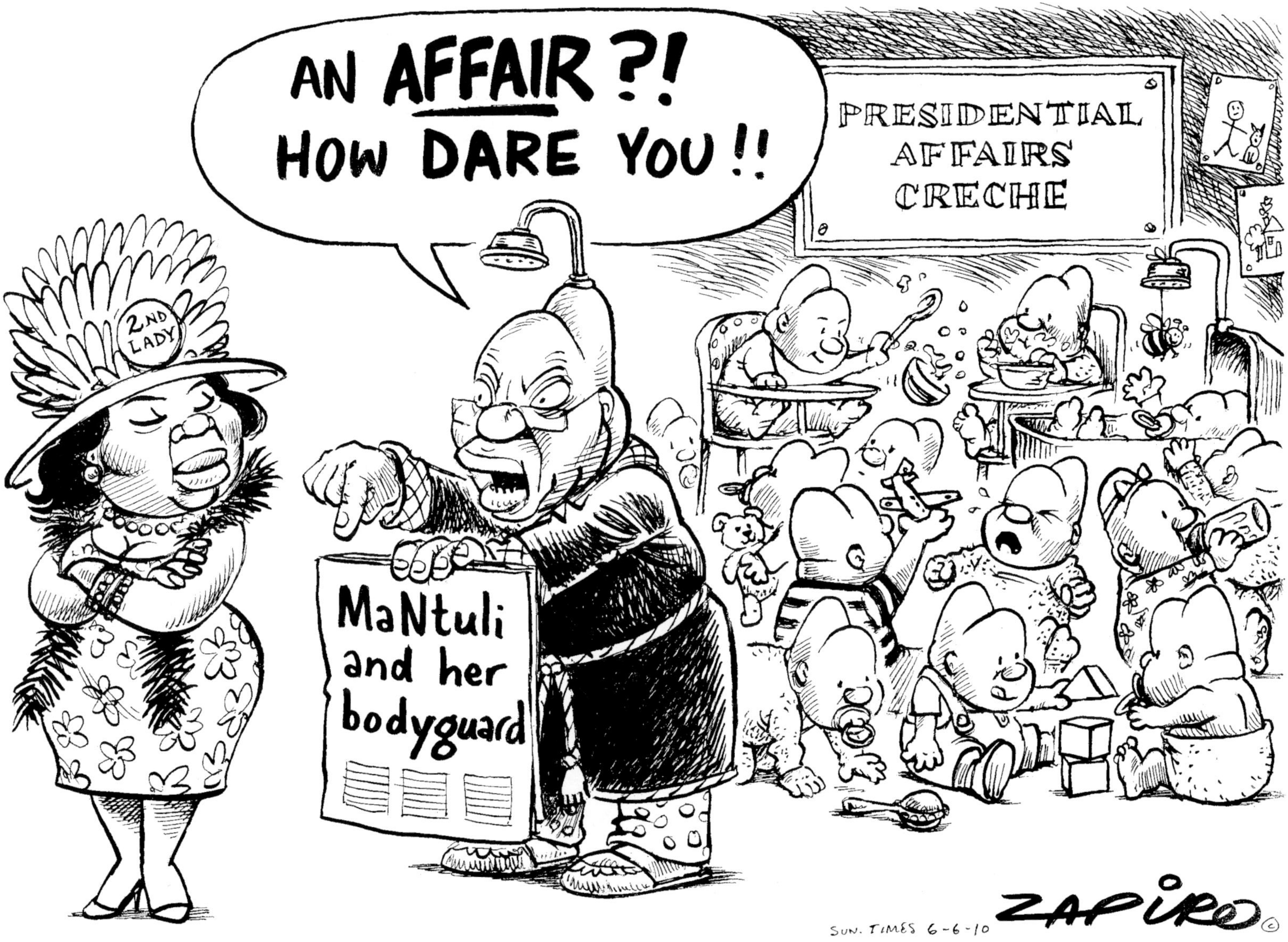
AN AFFAIR?! HOW DARE YOU!!
PRESIDENTIAL AFFAIRS CRECHE
2ND LADY
MaNtuli and her bodyguard
ZAPIRO
SUN. TIMES 6-6-10

6 June 2010

Cape Town's toilet saga: instead of communal toilets, the city gave each household in Makhaza, Khayelitsha, an open toilet to be enclosed by the owner. Yuk.

8 June 2010

Zwelinzima Vavi to face ANC discipline for criticising Zuma's failure to act on corruption allegations against his ministers

10 June 2010

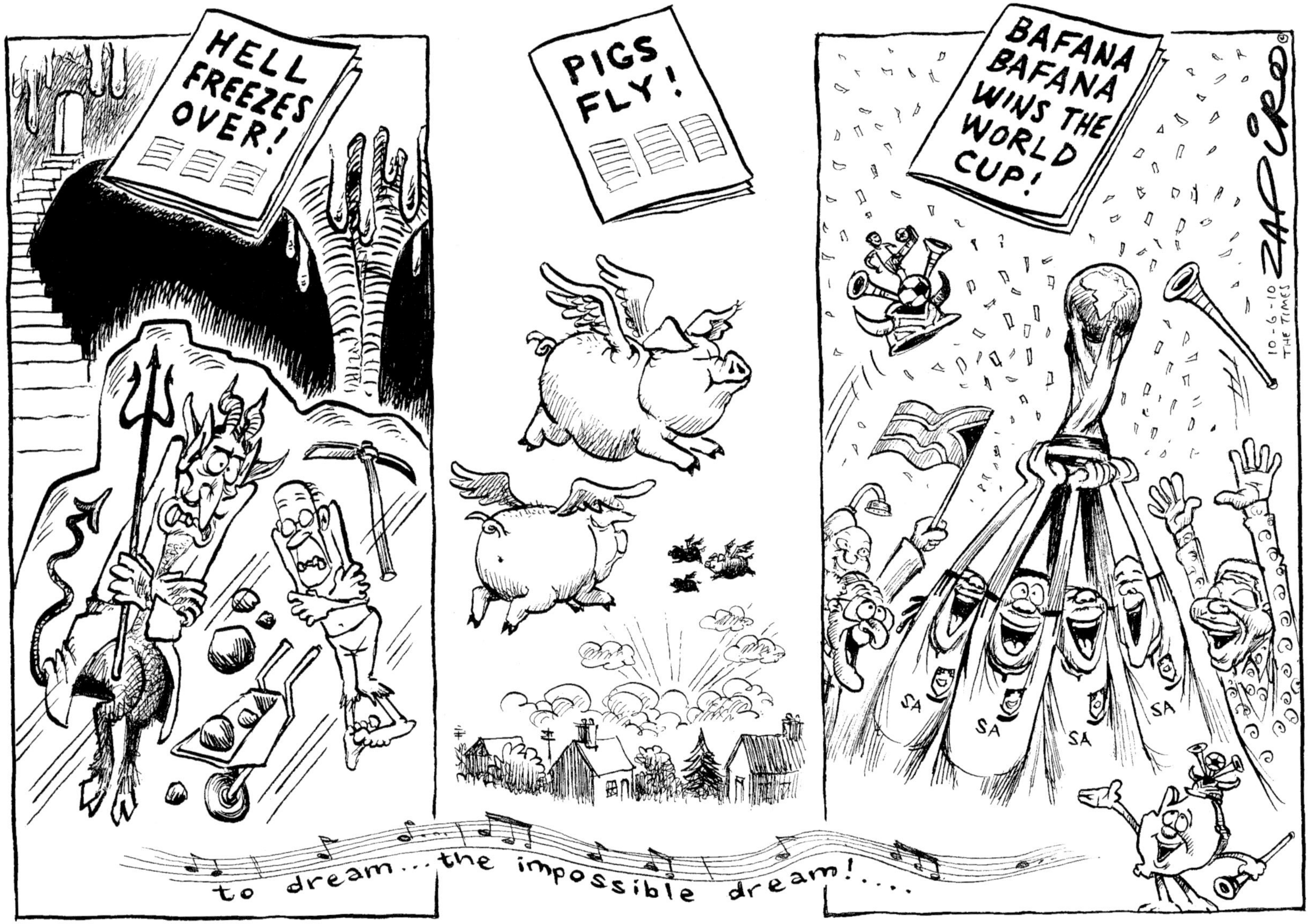
HELL FREEZES OVER!
PIGS FLY!
BAFANA BAFANA WINS THE WORLD CUP!
SA
SA
SA
SA
SA
to dream... the impossible dream!....
ZAPIRO
10-6-10 THE TIMES

10 June 2010

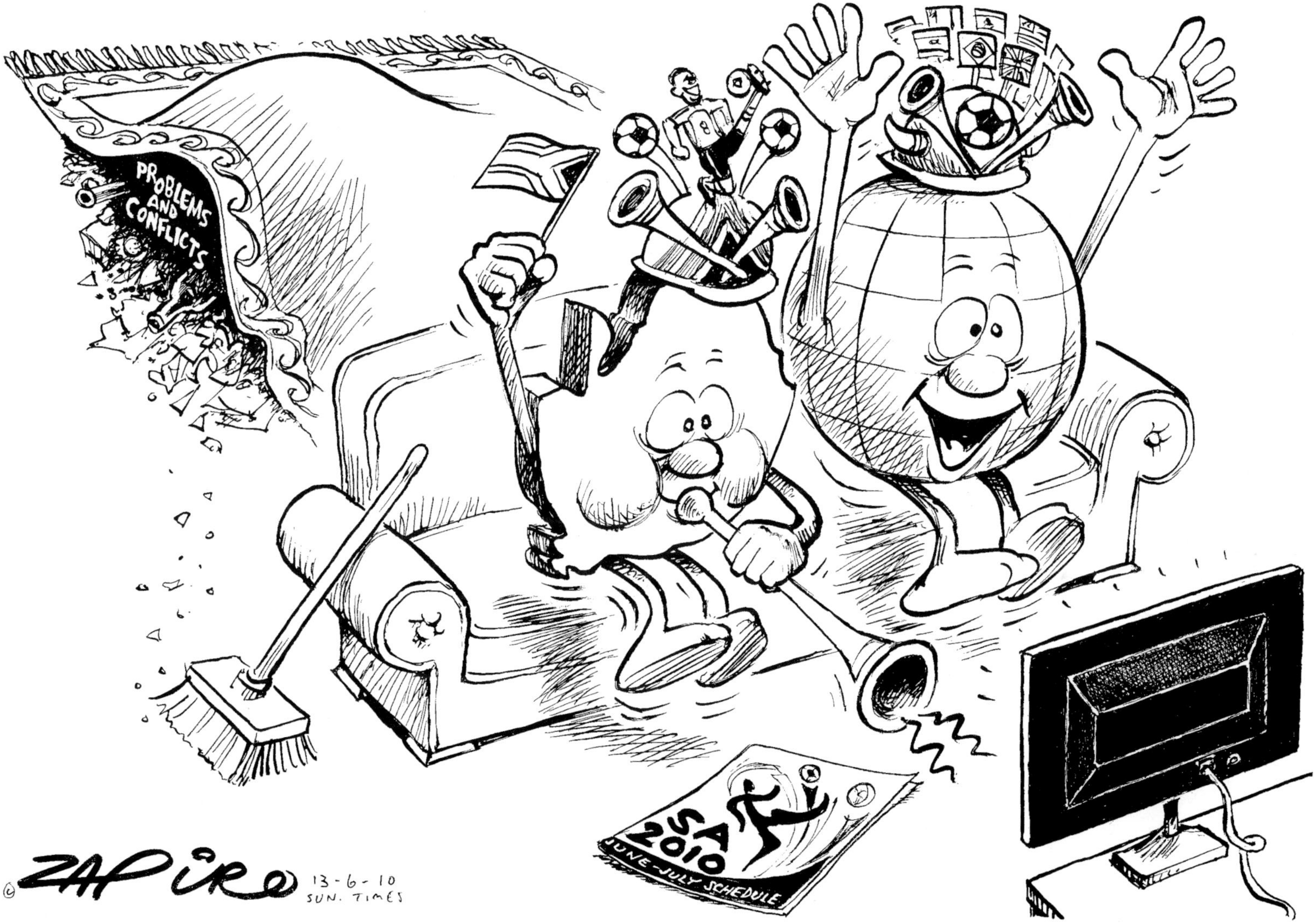
PROBLEMS AND CONFLICTS
SA 2010
JUNE-JULY SCHEDULE
© ZAPIRO 13-6-10 SUN. TIMES

13 June 2010

Kick-off

There's been a clamour for technology to assist referees. Now Sepp Blatter apologises to England and Mexico, both eliminated after refereeing blunders.

1 July 2010

1 July 2010

Ghana's Black Stars are the youngest team at SA 2010 and the only African team to reach the knockout stage. South Africans rally in support.

Africa wuz robbed! Deliberate two-handed handball by Uruguayan forward Luis Suarez prevents the goal that should have taken Ghana to the semi-finals.

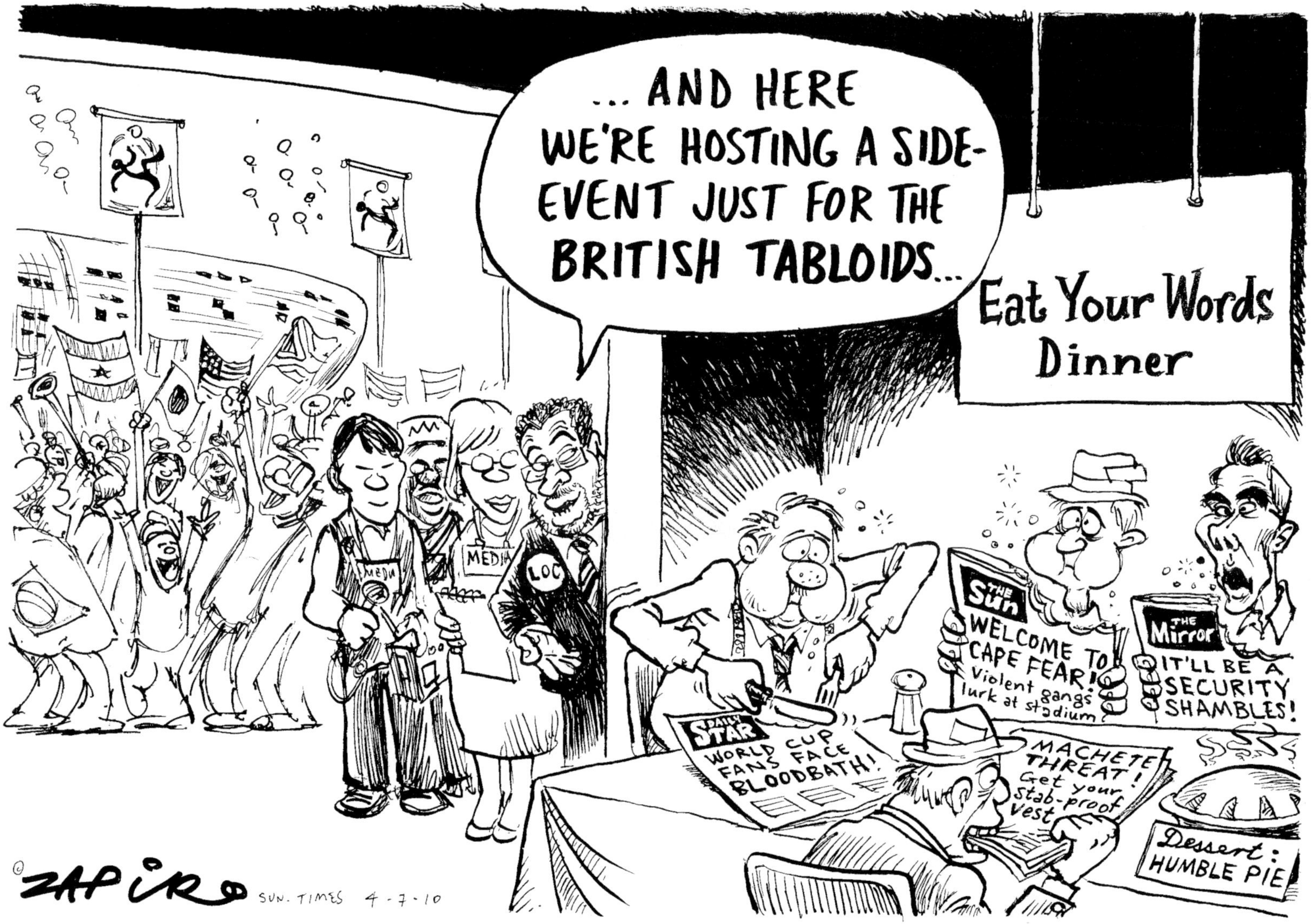
... AND HERE WE'RE HOSTING A SIDE-EVENT JUST FOR THE BRITISH TABLOIDS...
Eat Your Words Dinner
MEDIA
MEDIA
LOC
THE Sun
WELCOME TO CAPE FEAR!
Violent gangs lurk at stadium
THE Mirror
IT'LL BE A SECURITY SHAMBLES!
DAILY STAR
WORLD CUP FANS FACE BLOODBATH!
MACHETE THREAT! Get your stab-proof vest
Dessert: HUMBLE PIE
© ZAPIRO SUN. TIMES 4-7-10

4 July 2010

Chilling report that some Jo'burg township dwellers will attack others seen as foreigners as soon as the World Cup is over

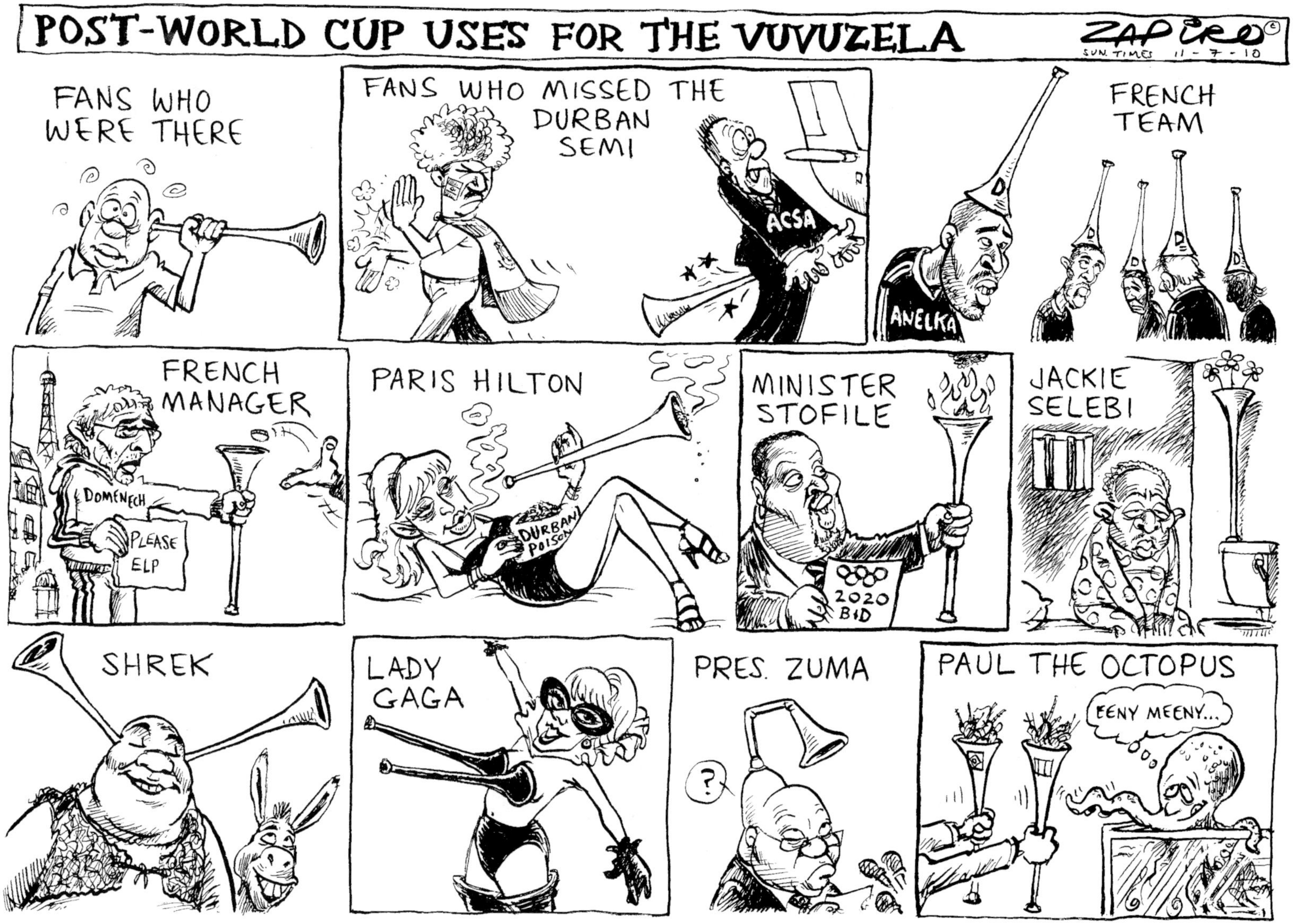
POST-WORLD CUP USES FOR THE VUVUZELA
ZAPIRO
SUN. TIMES 11-7-10
FANS WHO WERE THERE
FANS WHO MISSED THE DURBAN SEMI
ACSA
FRENCH TEAM
ANELKA
D
FRENCH MANAGER
DOMENECH
PLEASE ELP
PARIS HILTON
DURBAN POISON
MINISTER STOFILE
2020 BID
JACKIE SELEBI
SHREK
LADY GAGA
PRES. ZUMA
?
PAUL THE OCTOPUS
EENY MEENY...

11 July 2010

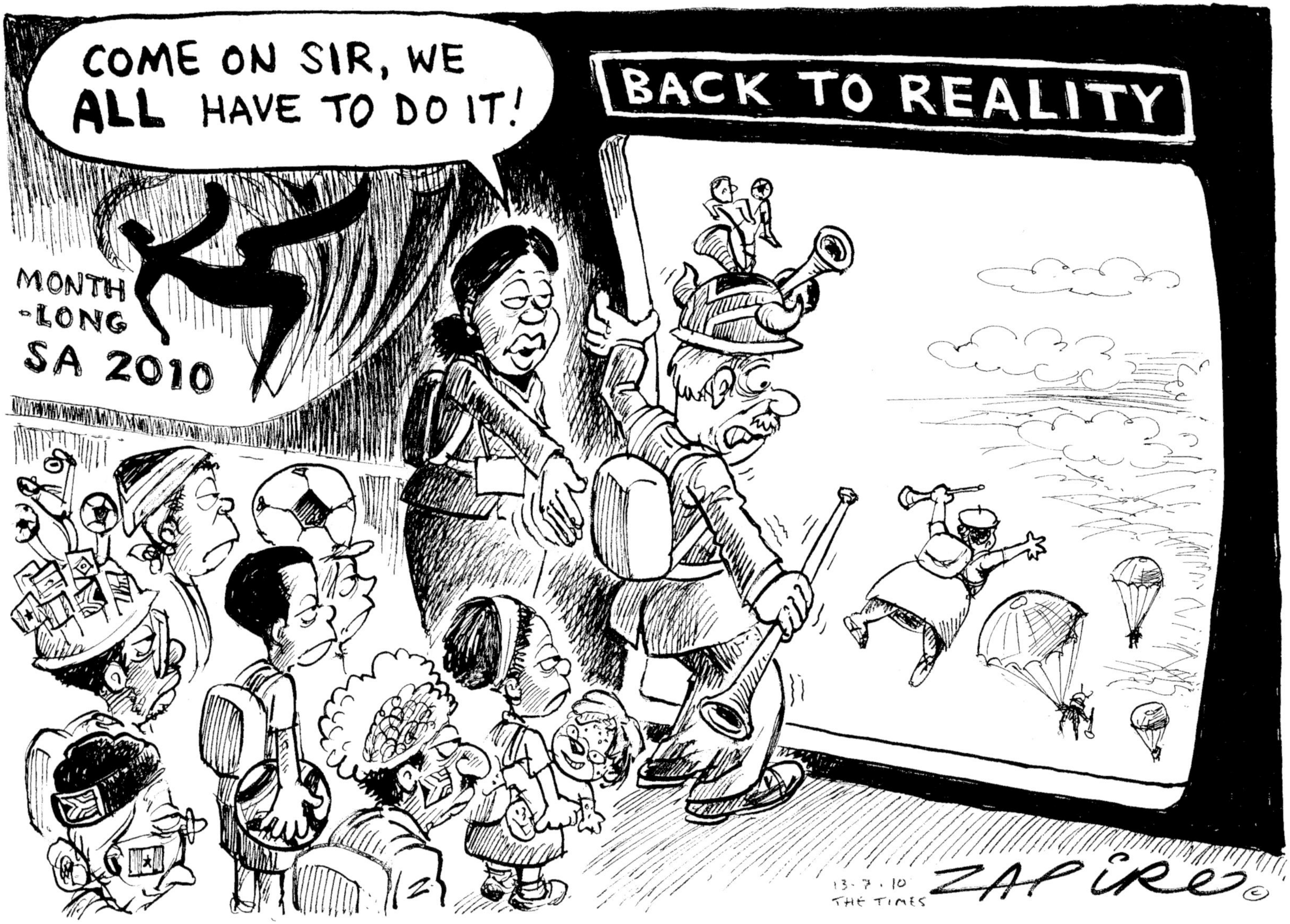
COME ON SIR, WE ALL HAVE TO DO IT!
BACK TO REALITY
MONTH -LONG SA 2010
13-7-10 THE TIMES
ZAPIRO ©

13 July 2010

Fears of post-World Cup xenophobic attacks turn to reality in Jo'burg and Cape Town. Thousands of foreigners flee.

15 July 2010

18 July 2010 — For the 2nd year, people give '67 minutes for Mandela' on his birthday

15 July 2010 — Rev Mvume Dandala quits

Allegation that the former Western Cape premier paid journalists to ensure favourable coverage should, but doesn't, scupper his appointment

8 July 2010

If this bill becomes a law, it'll mean draconian prison sentences for publishing or even possessing info deemed classified by all sorts of officials

20 July 2010

22 July 2010 … and the ANC also wants the press to be policed by a media tribunal answerable to Parliament

25 July 2010   The Arch announces he'll retire from public life in three months' time when he turns 79

Applause for new South African Airways chair Cheryl Carolus who aims to recover R27 million when SAA sues axed CEO Khaya Ngula for misspending R31 million

22 July 2010

Communications Minister Siphiwe Nyanda looks to be benefiting improperly from contracts tendered through his ministry

27 July 2010

29 July 2010

Panic as 'pet' tiger Panjo escapes near Delmas in Mpumalanga. Springbok world-beaters have slumped to three thrashings by New Zealand and Australia.

Trial of druglord Glenn Agliotti for the murder of Brett Kebble. Kebble's 'assisted suicide' narrated by a procession of self-confessed hitmen singing for indemnity.

29 July 2010

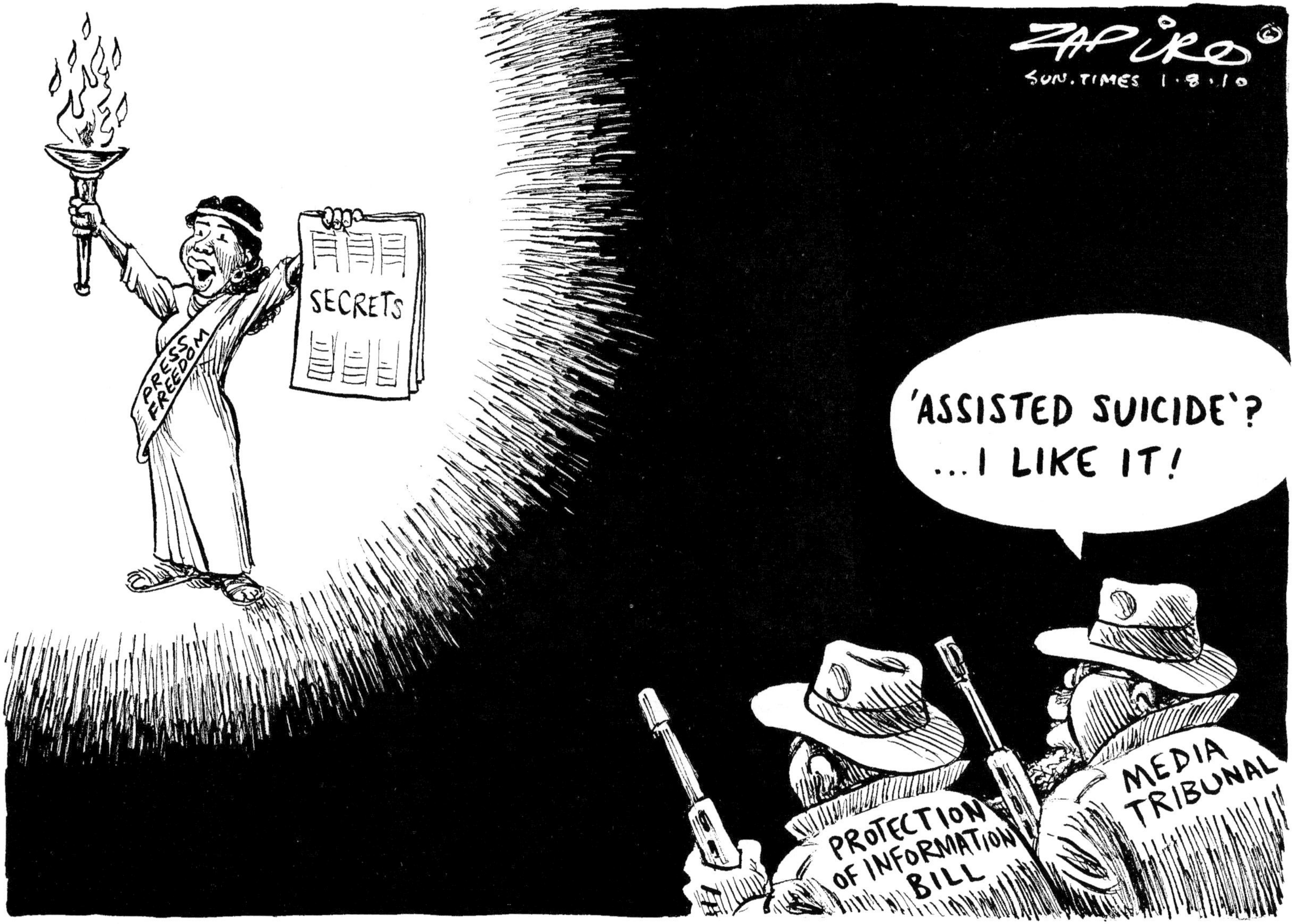
ZAPIRO©
SUN.TIMES 1·8·10
SECRETS
PRESS FREEDOM
'ASSISTED SUICIDE'?
...I LIKE IT!
PROTECTION OF INFORMATION BILL
MEDIA TRIBUNAL

1 August 2010

Media exposé: Bheki Cele signed a lease for a new HQ without tendering, two months before the ANC-linked seller owned the building

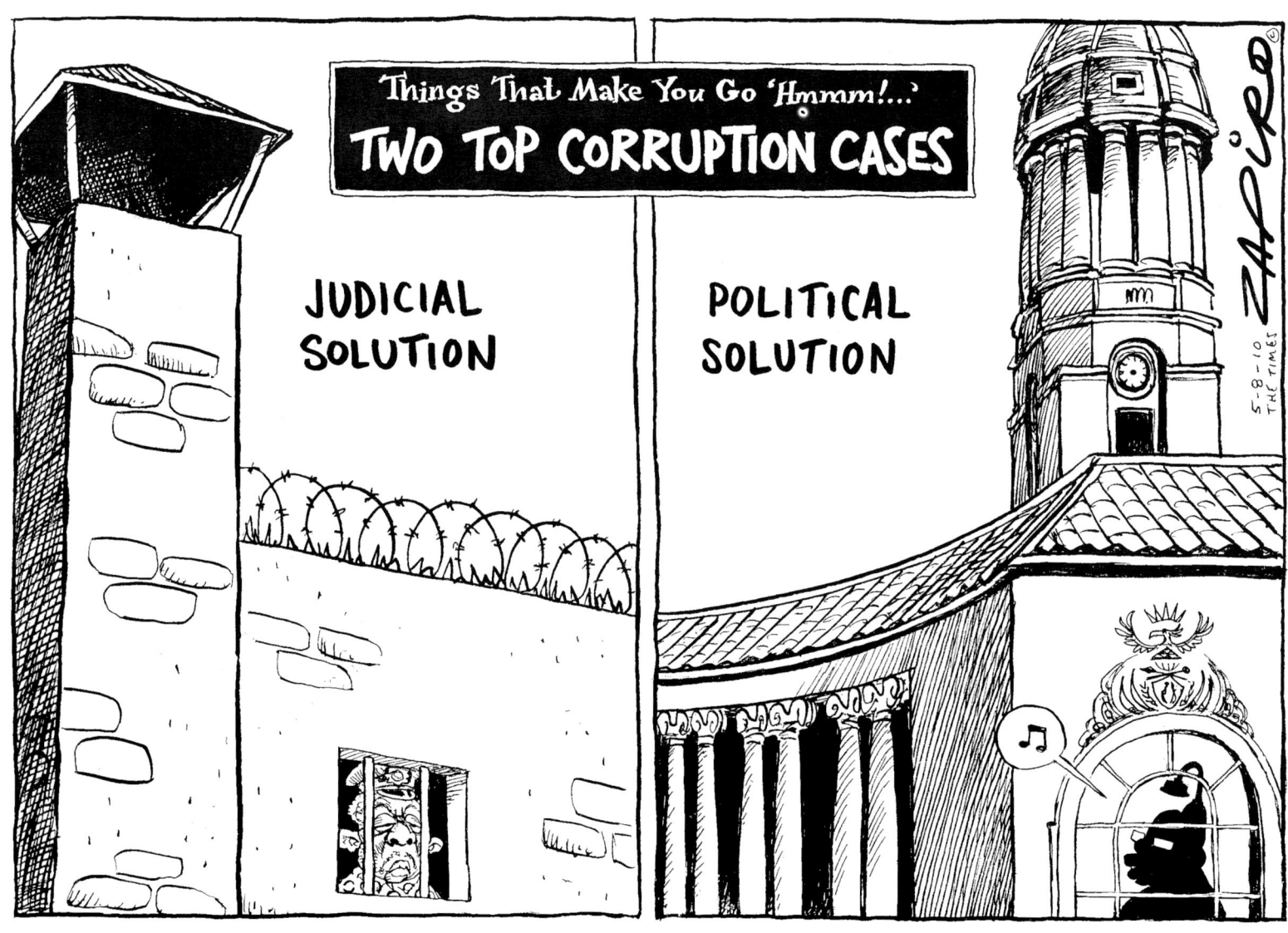

5 August 2010 — Selebi sentenced to 15 years

5 August 2010 — If it weren't for the *Mail & Guardian*, Selebi might never have been charged

Fears for the media as the Hawks arrest Mzilikazi wa Afrika, the *Sunday Times* reporter behind the exposé on General Cele

8 August 2010

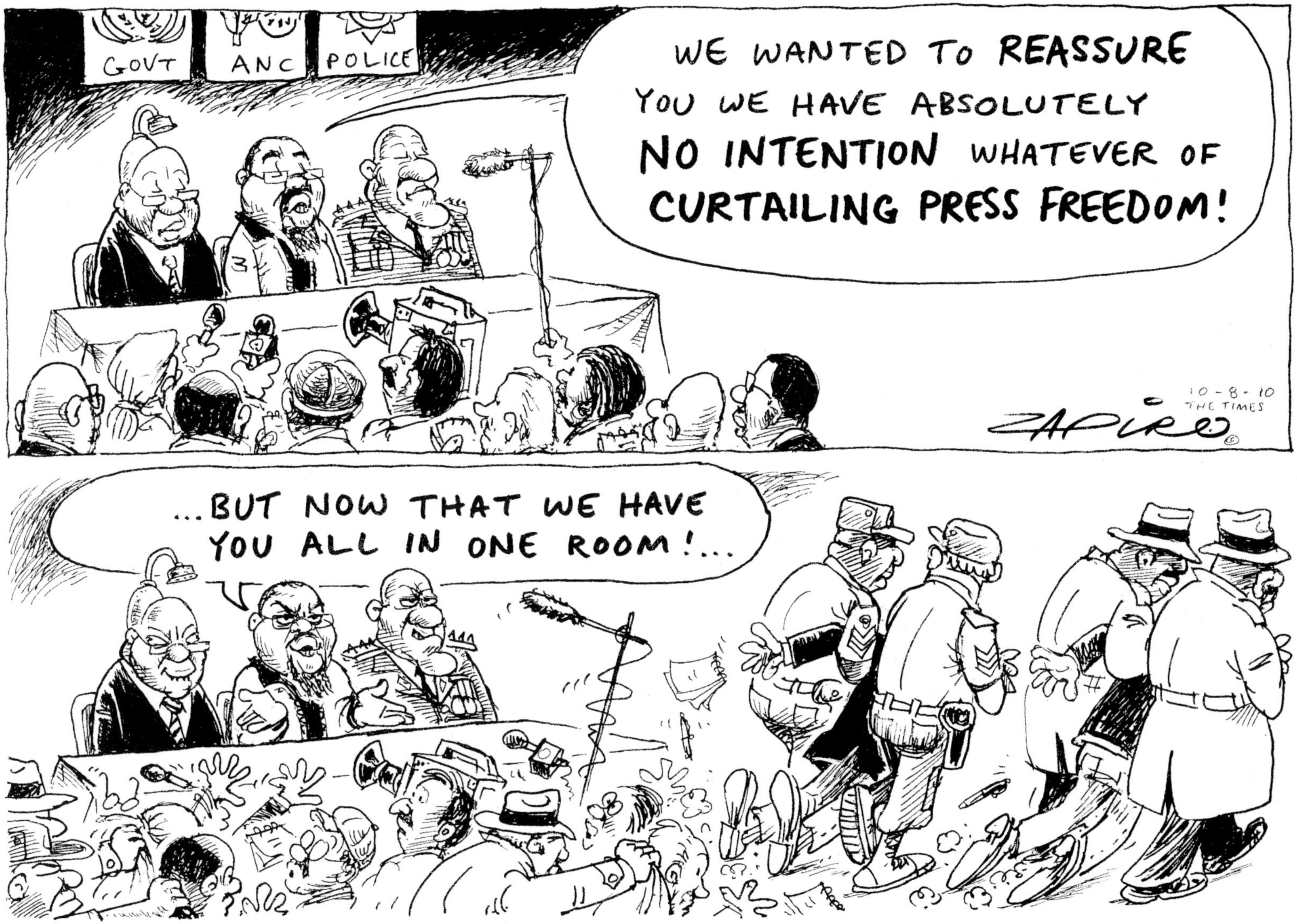
GOVT
ANC
POLICE
WE WANTED TO REASSURE YOU WE HAVE ABSOLUTELY NO INTENTION WHATEVER OF CURTAILING PRESS FREEDOM!
10-8-10
THE TIMES
ZAPIRO
...BUT NOW THAT WE HAVE YOU ALL IN ONE ROOM!...

10 August 2010

Press briefing

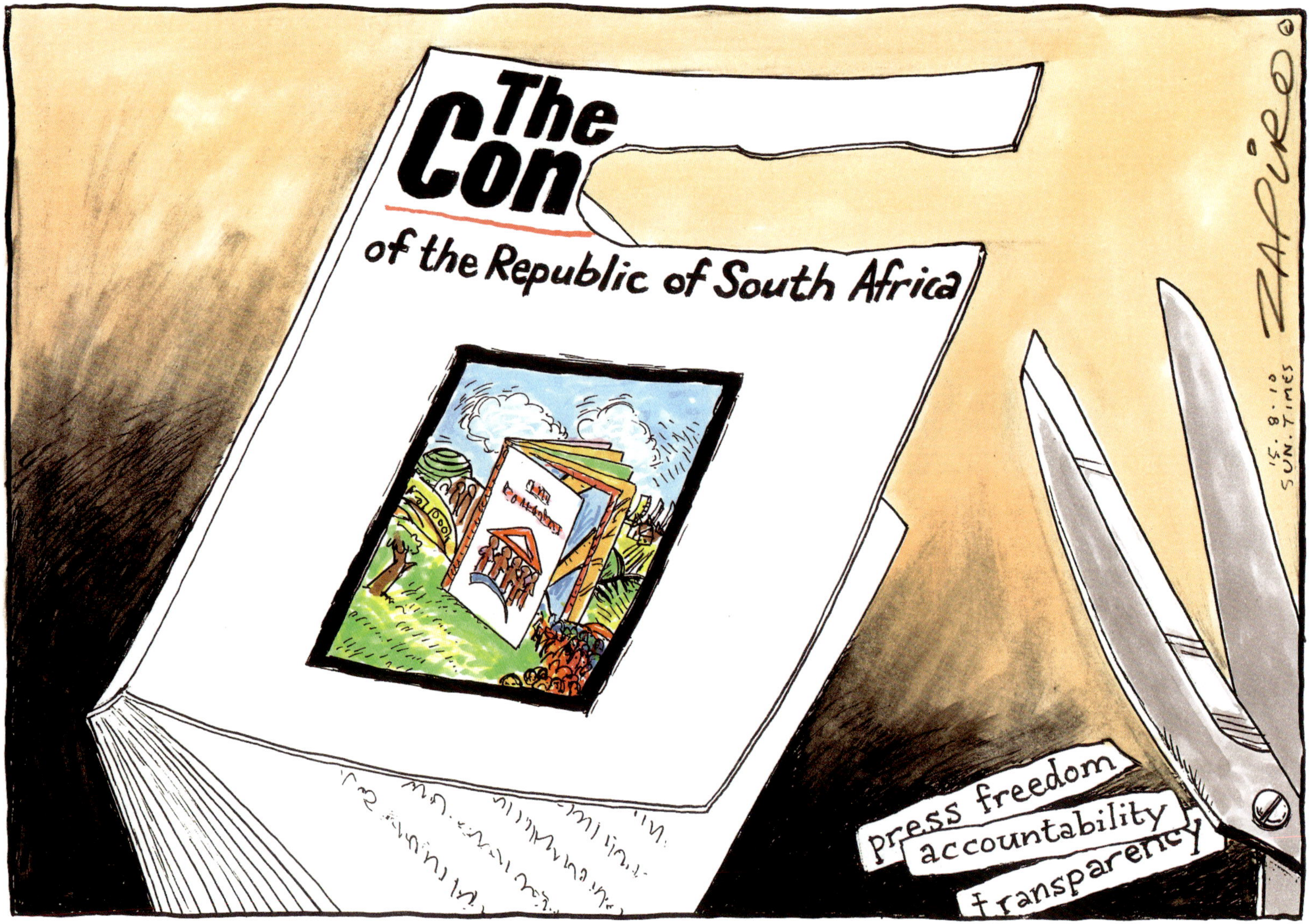
The Con
of the Republic of South Africa
press freedom
accountability
transparency
ZAPIRO
15.8.10
SUN. TIMES

15 August 2010

Zuma slams the media for negativity. Meanwhile the new ANC-aligned newspaper funded by Zuma's friends, the Gupta family, is soon to be launched.

19 August 2010

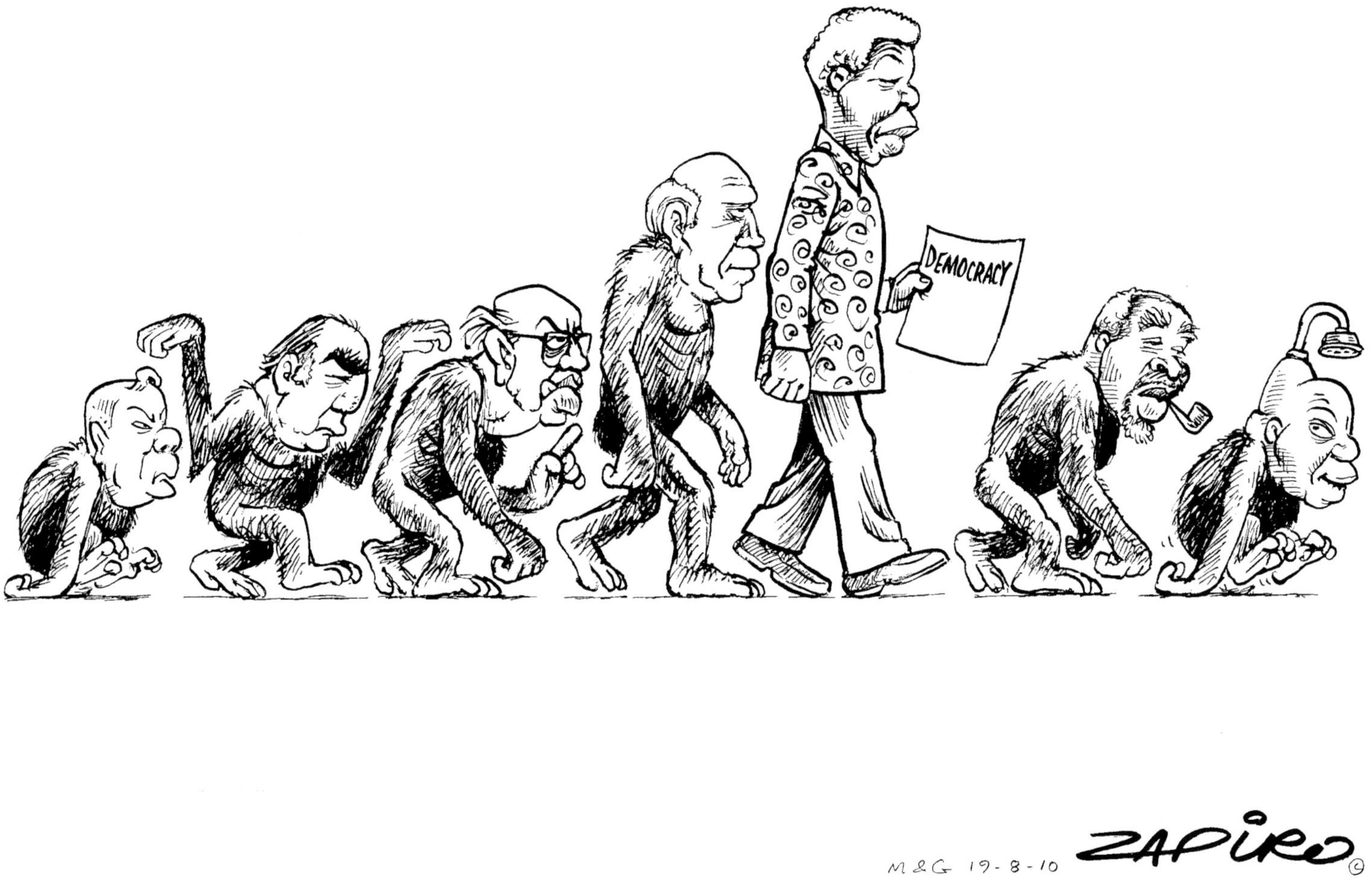
DEMOCRACY
M&G 19-8-10
ZAPIRO ©

19 August 2010

At the war crimes trial in the Netherlands of former Liberian ruler Charles Taylor, reluctant witness Naomi Campbell says she didn't know the dirty stones he gave her in 1997 were diamonds. Hmmm …

12 August 2010

Seeking wider appeal, Helen Zille's Democratic Alliance merges with Patricia de Lille's much smaller Independent Democrats

22 August 2010 — Public servants' strike turns ugly

24 August 2010 — Cape Town's Athlone cooling towers are demolished due to structural deterioration

Delivering the Ruth First Memorial Lecture, Vavi says the Info bill mocks what she stood for as a journalist, and she'd be rolling in her grave at the new crass materialism and graft

26 August 2010

7 September 2010

Zuma's son Duduzane will clear R900 million in the Arcelor-Mittal deal, his nephew Khulubuse has amassed billions in DRC oil deals, and the list goes on

29 August 2010 — In China to promote SA business

31 August 2010

SABC board suspends CEO Solly Mokoetle, lobbies to axe chairman Ben Ngubane, is depleted by members quitting, and so on …

Anger at Springbok coach Peter de Villiers for knee-jerk support of the Blue Bulls prop arrested for allegedly killing Tshwane metro policeman Johannes Mogale with his bare hands

2 September 2010

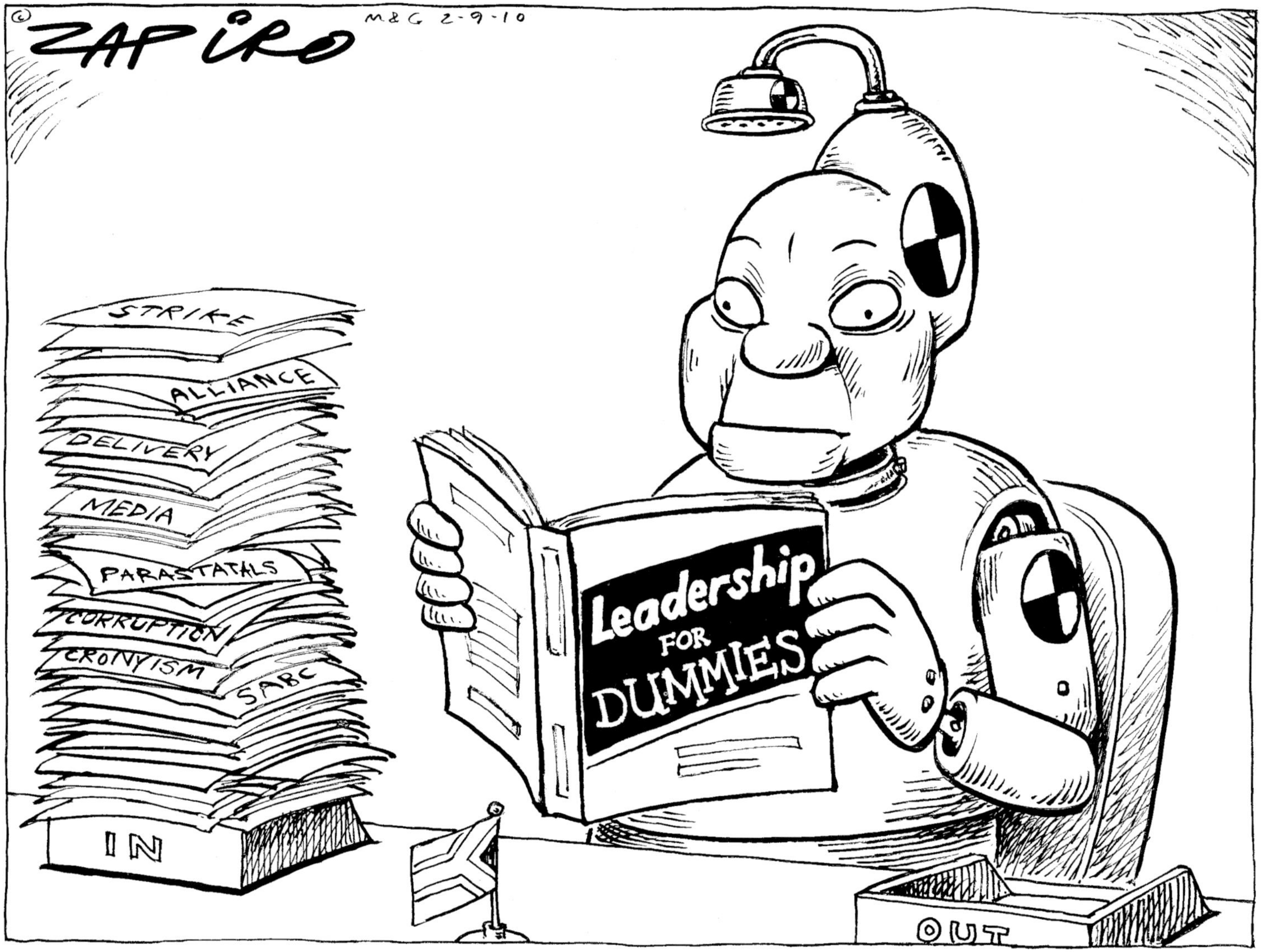
© ZAPIRO
M&G 2-9-10
STRIKE
ALLIANCE
DELIVERY
MEDIA
PARASTATALS
CORRUPTION
CRONYISM
SABC
IN
Leadership
FOR
DUMMIES
OUT

2 September 2010

He once said stopping Zuma from becoming president would be like trying to stop a tsunami. Now he lambastes the predator state run by corrupt political hyenas.

There's R480 million of arms deal payments still to probe but Hawks head Anwar Dramat wants to drop the whole thing. Well, with 460 boxes of documents and 4.7 million computer documents of evidence and just one investigator on the job …

9 September 2010

9 September 2010

When the NPA drops charges against Wa Afrika, an apology is demanded from Cele, while police generals say he lied to Parliament about his lease agreement

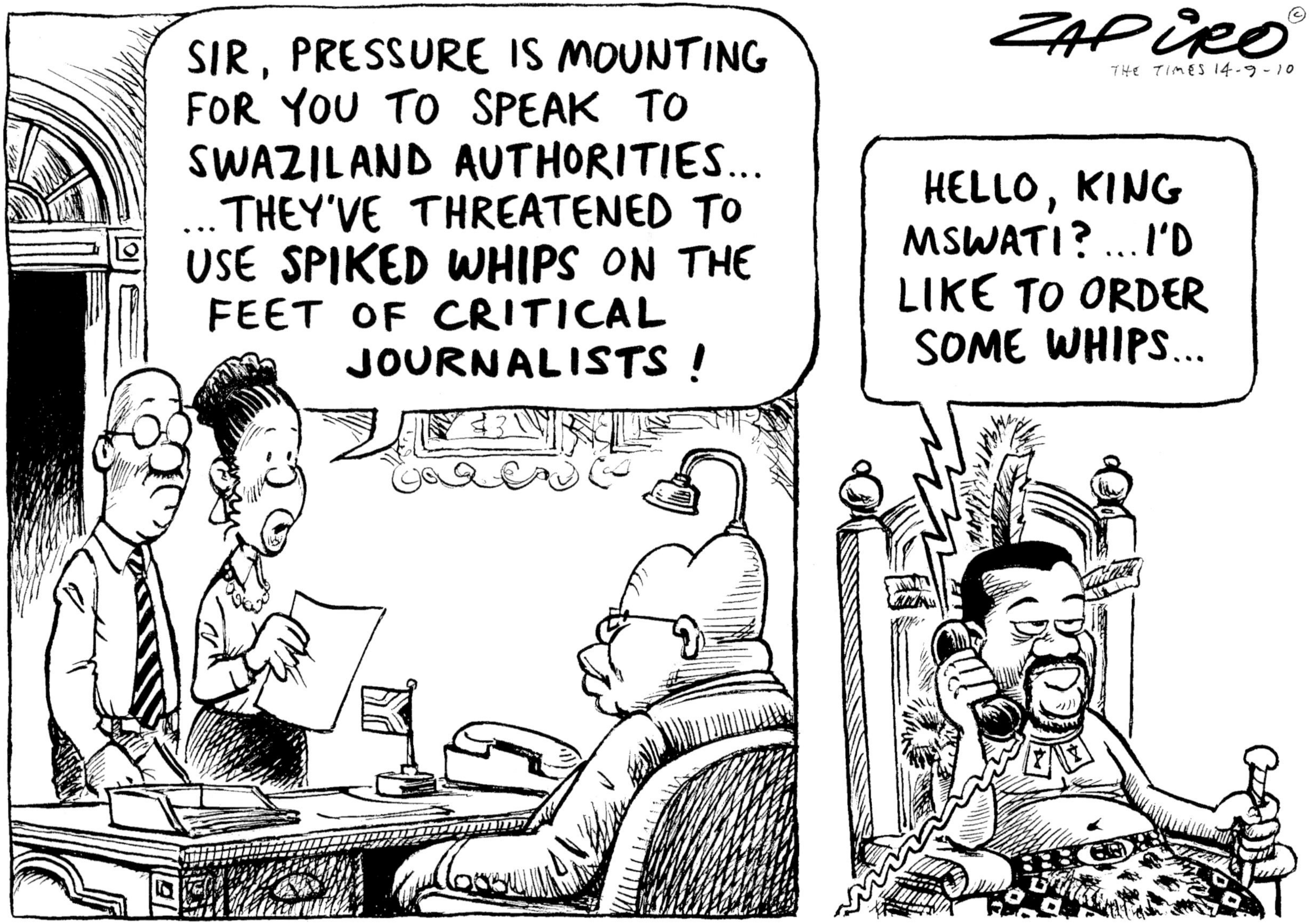
SIR, PRESSURE IS MOUNTING FOR YOU TO SPEAK TO SWAZILAND AUTHORITIES... ...THEY'VE THREATENED TO USE SPIKED WHIPS ON THE FEET OF CRITICAL JOURNALISTS!
HELLO, KING MSWATI? ...I'D LIKE TO ORDER SOME WHIPS...
ZAPIRO ©
THE TIMES 14-9-10

14 September 2010

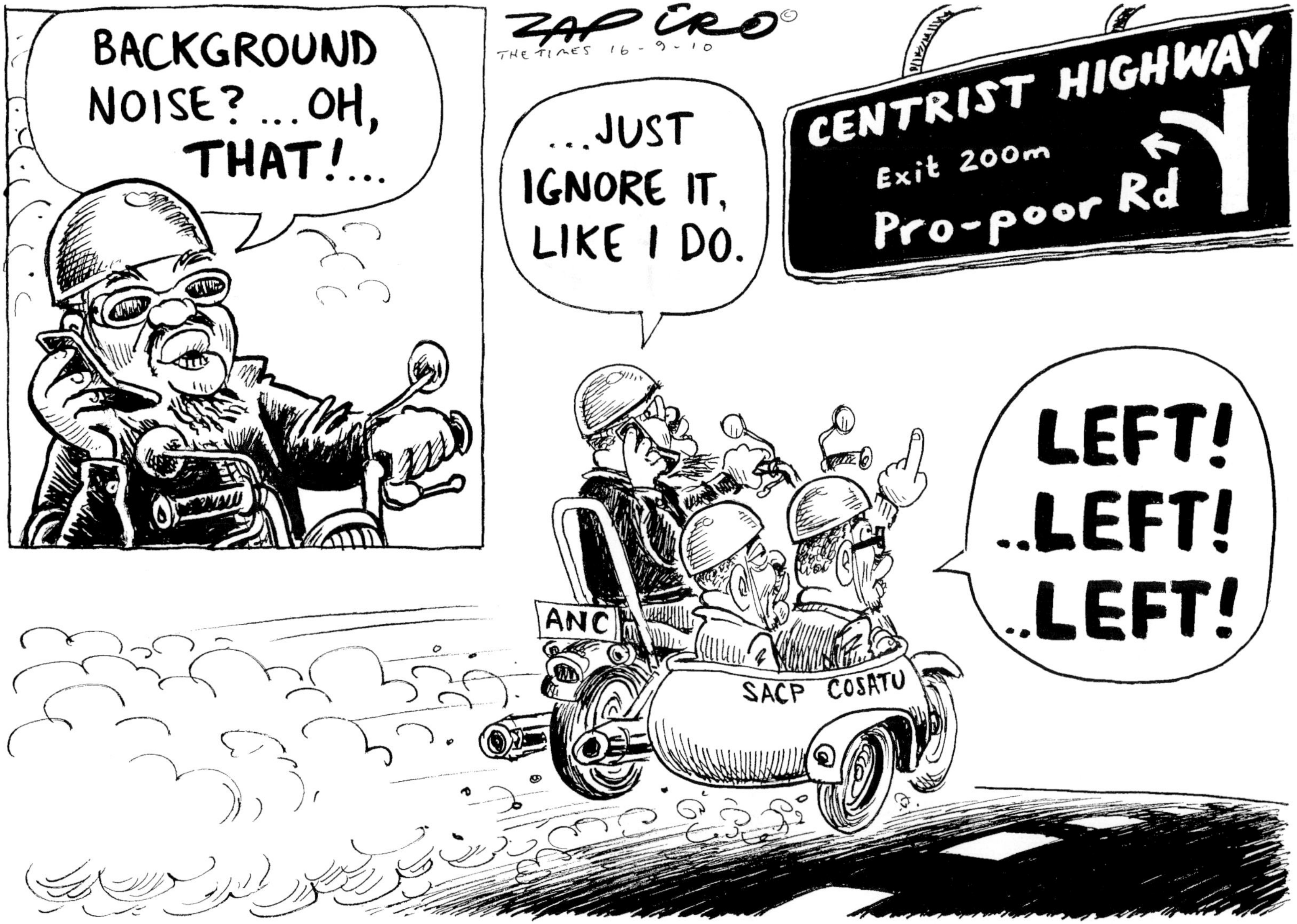
BACKGROUND NOISE? ...OH, THAT!...
ZAPIRO©
THE TIMES 16-9-10
...JUST IGNORE IT, LIKE I DO.
CENTRIST HIGHWAY
Exit 200m
Pro-poor Rd
LEFT! ..LEFT! ..LEFT!
ANC
SACP
COSATU

16 September 2010

Launching its alternative economic policy, Cosatu calls for nationalisation of key sectors and a tax on the super-rich

Pastor Terry Jones, leader of a small anti-Islamic church in Florida, plans to burn copies of the Qur'an on the anniversary of the September 11 attacks

12 September 2010

Obama brokers peace talks in Jerusalem. Netanyahu says the partial freeze on settlements is about to end. Abbas says in that case, so are the talks.

16 September 2010

French President Nicolas Sarkozy insists the expulsion of Roma people is to curb crime. Just as the burka ban was to help women.

19 September 2010

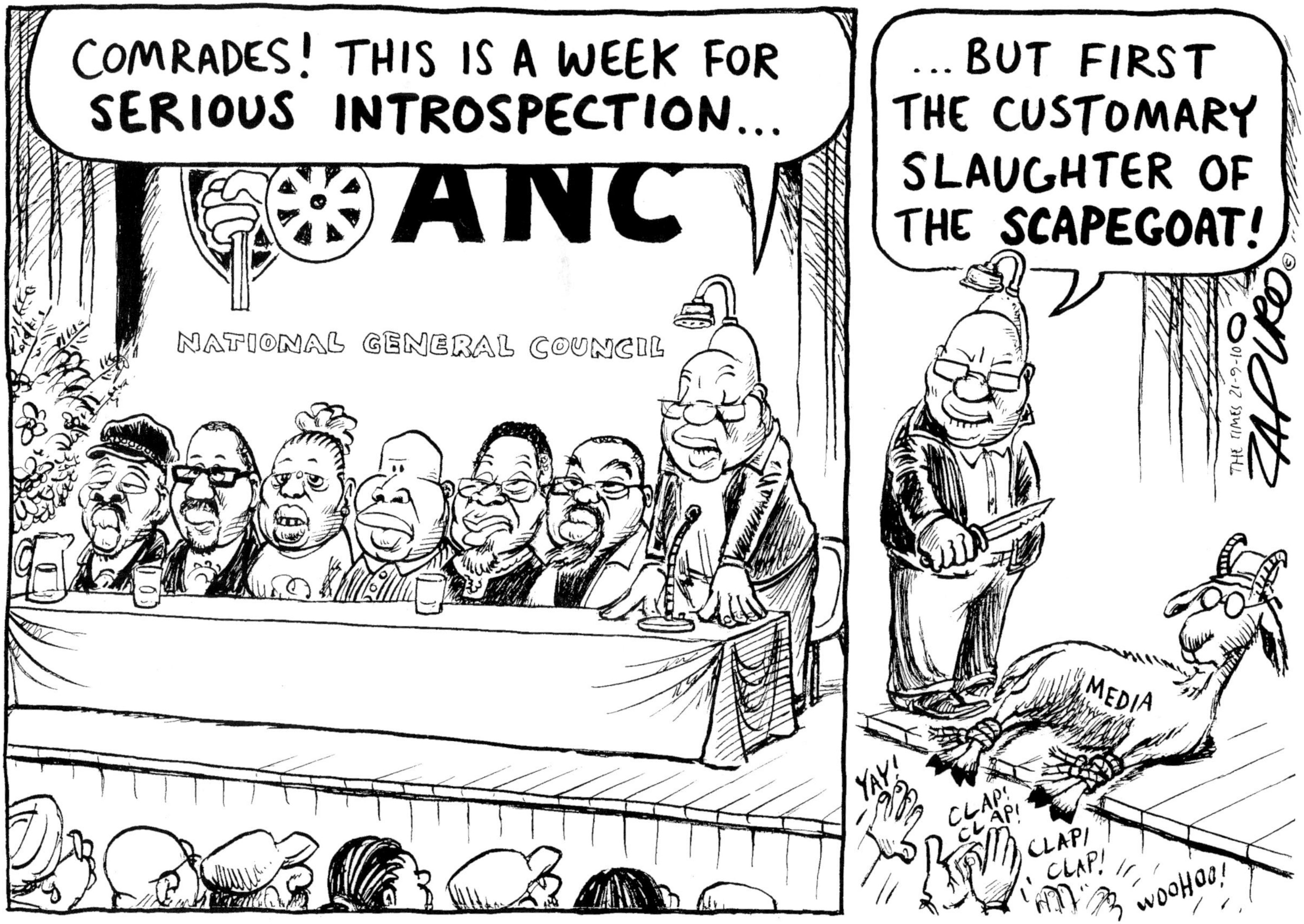
COMRADES! THIS IS A WEEK FOR SERIOUS INTROSPECTION...
ANC
NATIONAL GENERAL COUNCIL
...BUT FIRST THE CUSTOMARY SLAUGHTER OF THE SCAPEGOAT!
MEDIA
YAY!
CLAP! CLAP!
CLAP! CLAP!
WOOHOO!
ZAPIRO ©
THE TIMES 21-9-10

21 September 2010

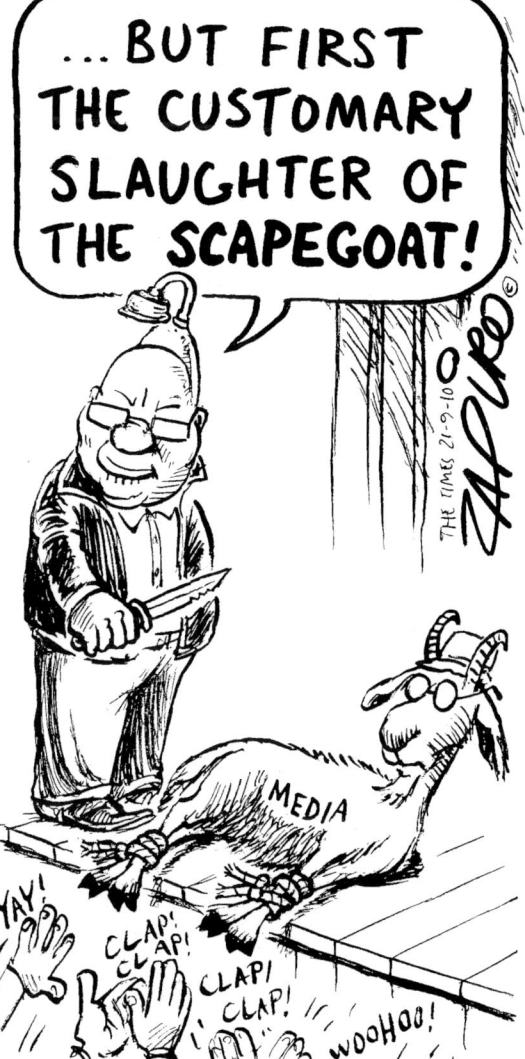

Problem-packed agenda in Durban

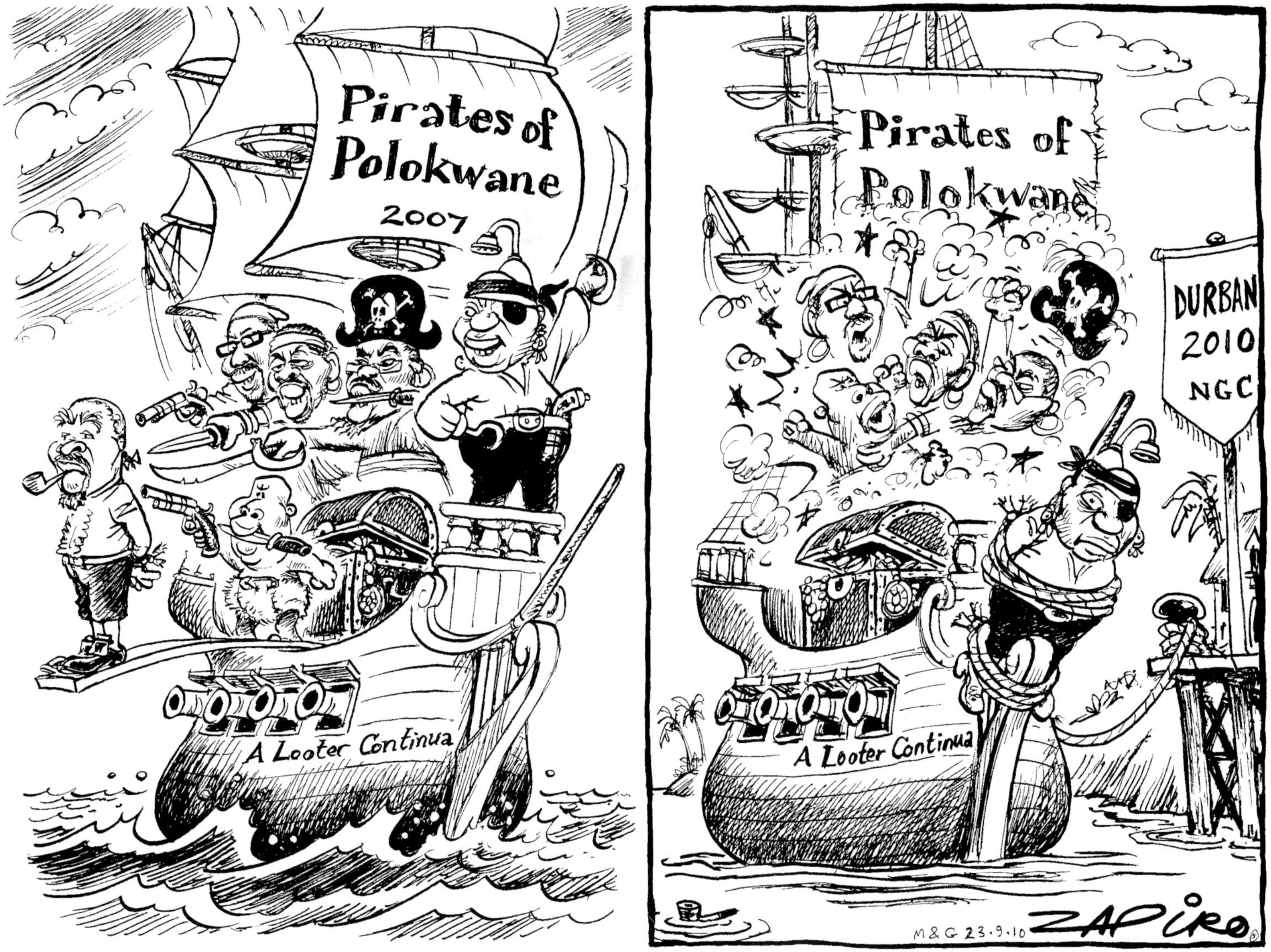
Pirates of Polokwane
2007
A Looter Continua
Pirates of Polokwane
DURBAN
2010
NGC
A Looter Continua
M&G 23.9.10
ZAPIRO

23 September 2010

23 September 2010

His opening speech includes a sharp dressing-down of the Youth League and a warning on ill-discipline

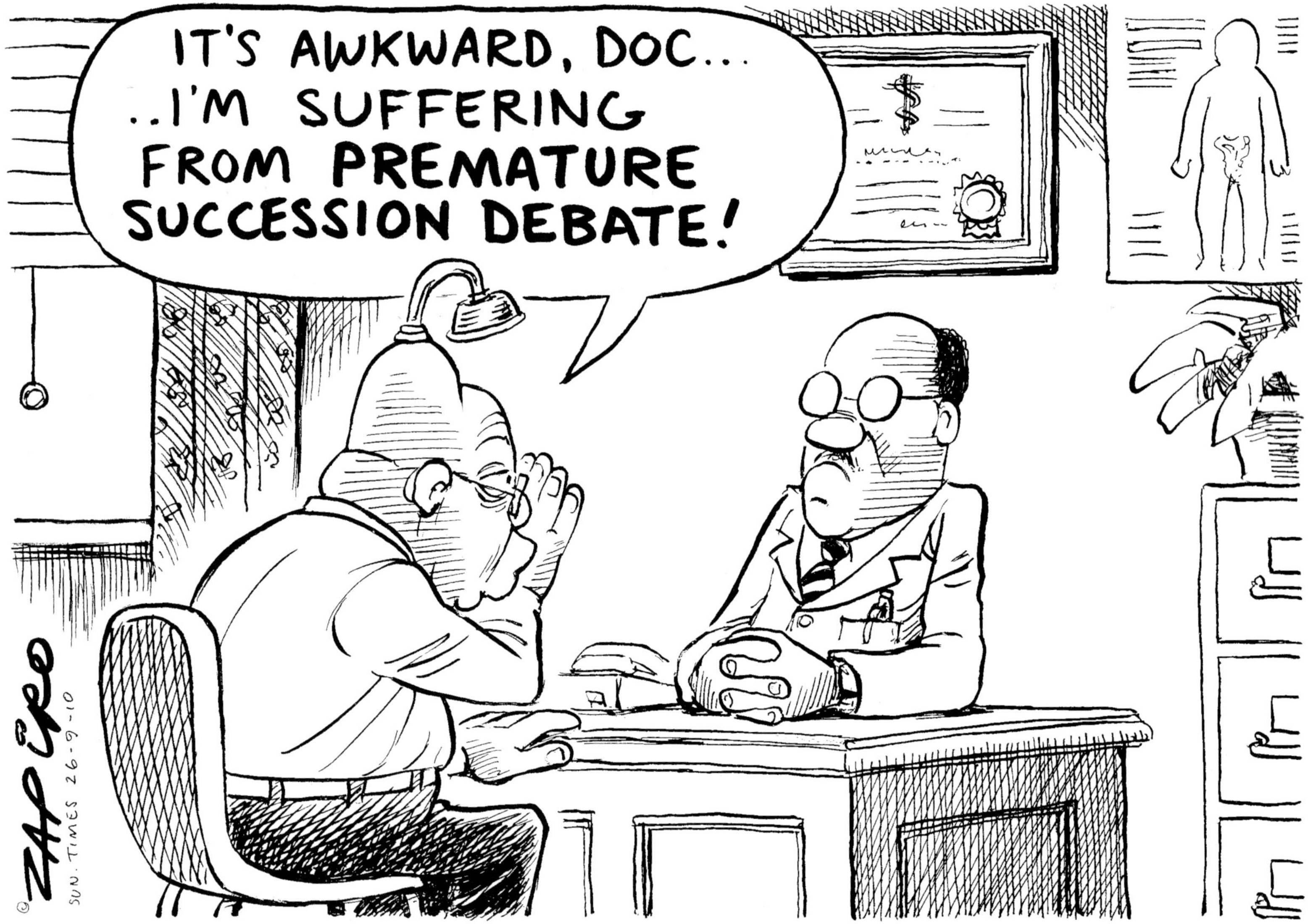
IT'S AWKWARD, DOC...
..I'M SUFFERING FROM PREMATURE SUCCESSION DEBATE!
© ZAPIRO SUN. TIMES 26-9-10

26 September 2010